RYA
Wing & Windsurfing
for Instructors

© RYA
Second Edition 2024
Previously published as the RYA Windsurfing Instructor Manual
The Royal Yachting Association
RYA House, Ensign Way,
Hamble, Southampton,
Hampshire SO31 4YA

Tel: 02380 604 100

Web: www.rya.org.uk

We welcome feedback on our publications at publications@rya.org.uk

You can check content updates for RYA publications at
www.rya.org.uk/go/bookschangelog

ISBN: 978-1-9100-17-29-6

Cover design: Pete Galvin
Illustrations: Pete Galvin
Photographic credits: Steve Gladders, with thanks to Keith Bow,
Christian Brown, Alain Cadoret, Fraser Green, Victoria Kirkland, Wayne Noble,
Lloyd Scott, Dan Van den Bosch; OTC, Sam Ross, Scotty Stallman
Acknowledgements: Tim Cross, James Hardy, Laurie MacDonald, David Mellor,
Nic Wymer
Typesetting and design: Velveo Design
Proofreading and indexing: David Gaskell
Printed in the UK

CONTENTS

FOREWORD

Wing and windsurfing are exhilarating and accessible. We are excited that you are taking the next step and either qualifying as an RYA Instructor or continuing your progression along the RYA pathway, helping to pass knowledge on to others and enabling them to enjoy and progress in these exciting sports.

Written as a companion for anyone from aspiring Instructors through to experienced Trainers, this book covers aspects of RYA Recognised Training Centre information, explanations of learning styles, and RYA teaching methods that accompany each level of these schemes.

In this book you will find suggested theory and practical-session guidance outlining step-by-step content for the RYA National and Youth Wing and Windsurfing Schemes. The book is not designed as a stand-alone Instructor manual and should be used in conjunction with other RYA scheme publications and the RYA website. Complementary scheme publications are listed in relevant chapters, along with links to useful webpages and external sites.

Happy teaching and hope to see you on the water.

Liz McMaster

RYA Chief Instructor – Dinghy, Wing & Windsurfing

RYA NATIONAL WINDSURFING SCHEME

The National Windsurfing Scheme

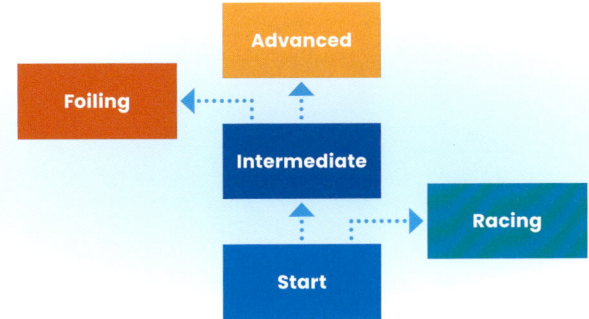

Within the National Windsurfing Scheme there are core courses (Start, Intermediate, and Advanced), with additional clinics concentrating on key skills (gybing, beachstarting, waterstarting etc). This ensures a tailored approach to an individual's needs and teaching environment.

The Youth Windsurfing Scheme directly relates to the National Windsurfing Scheme, providing ease of use and comparison. On completing Stage 4 your students should have the skill and ability to progress through the advanced courses and clinics of the National Windsurfing Scheme.

For information on assessing ability and teaching the different levels of the National and Youth Windsurfing Schemes, refer to page 64.

The Youth Windsurfing Scheme and its comparison to the National Scheme

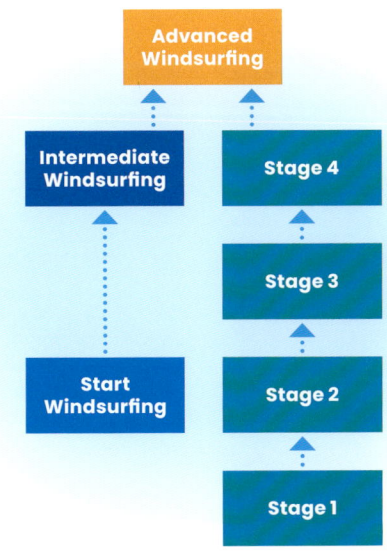

RYA WING SCHEME

Introduction

The concept of wing-powered watersports has been explored and trialled many times over the last forty years or so, but its ingenuity and appeal never really crystalised until 2018/2019, helped largely by the meteoric rise and influence of foiling.

Foiling has changed the landscape entirely. What is more, the use of wing power is one of the easiest and quickest methods of learning how to foil, attracting people from very different backgrounds.

The RYA Wing Scheme provides a great introduction to the sport, progressing on to foiling, undoubtedly opening doors to more time on the water.

With wingfoiling rapidly diversifying into many disciplines, it really can be the foiling sport for the masses. Whether you want to cruise on flat water, venture into downwinders, race, learn tricks, or ride swell and waves, the sport and kit can take you there.

The RYA Wing Scheme

The RYA Wing Scheme has four courses to help progress and develop into the sport:

1. Learn to Wingsurf (an introductory course, approximately four hours in duration):
   a. Flying the Wing Ashore
   b. Wingsurfing Afloat
2. Improve your Wingsurfing (building confidence and enhancing skills, approximately four hours in duration).
3. First Flights (Wingfoiling) (progress your skills and achieve your first flights. Eight to 10 hours, delivered over a number of short sessions or full days).
4. Sustained Flights (Wingfoiling) (advancing your skills, foiling knowledge, and sustaining flights. Eight to 10 hours, delivered over a number of short sessions or full days).

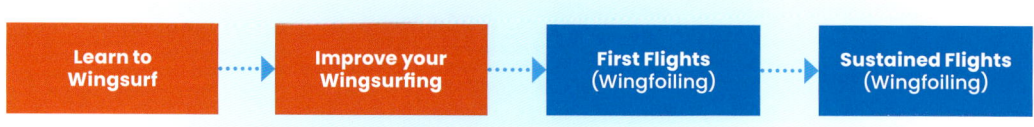

To aid progression through the RYA Wing scheme, and to simplify the teaching of the two disciplines, the RYA scheme and teaching sequence uses the following terms:

- **Wingsurfing:** Winging on a large windsurf board or stand-up paddleboard (SUP), non-foiling.
- **Wingfoiling:** Winging on a dedicated or dual-discipline foiling board.

RYA Wing Instructor Pathway

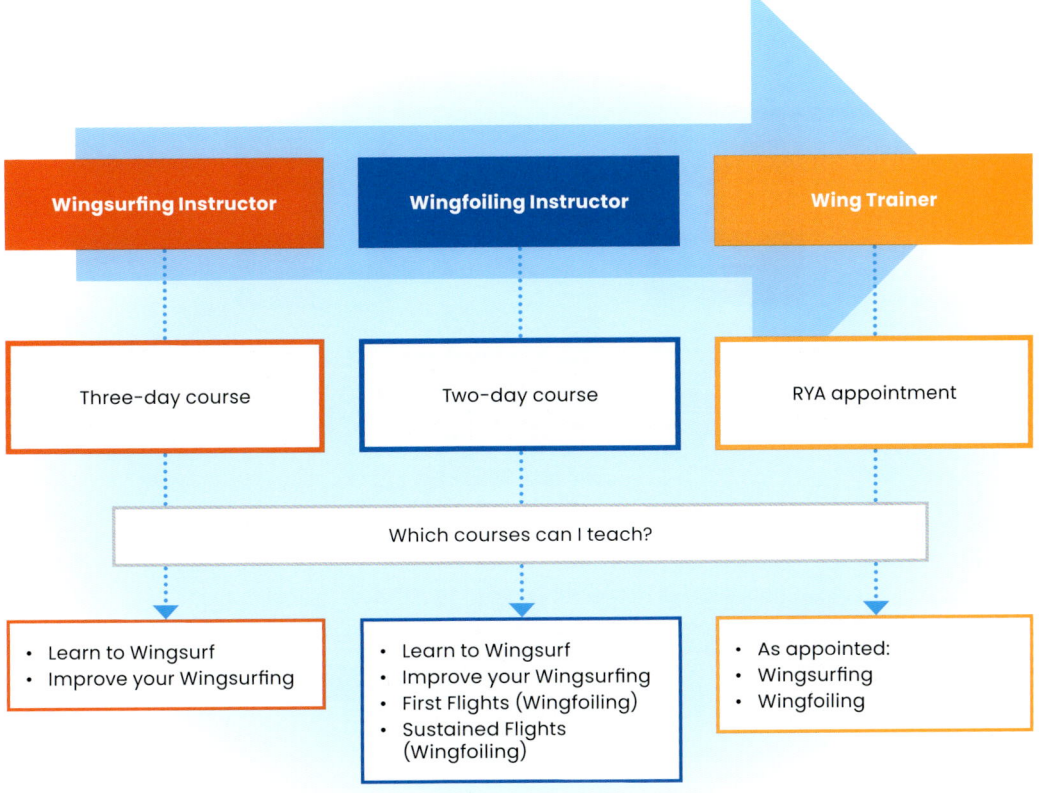

RYA INSTRUCTOR TRAINING AWARDS

RYA Windsurfing Instructor Pathway

There are designated Instructor pathways for both the training and racing schemes, each requiring different knowledge and experience.

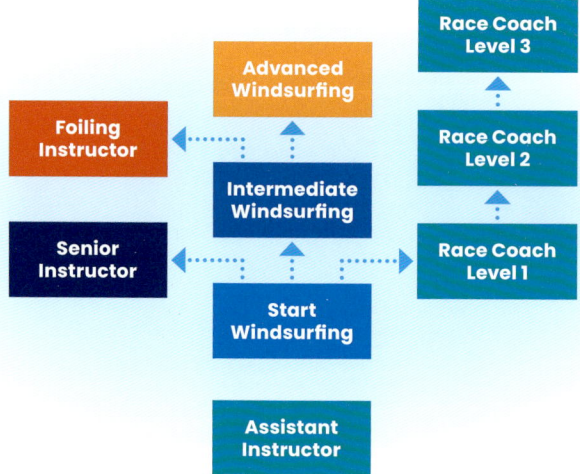

On successful completion of an RYA Instructor course the course Trainer will submit your information to the RYA Certification Department. Once processed, an Instructor certificate will be sent outlining the level of your Instructor qualification, basic terms, and the qualification expiry date.

Below is a list of useful RYA Publications available to assist you in your role as an Instructor:

- W1 RYA Youth Windsurfing Scheme Syllabus & Logbook
- G47 RYA National Windsurfing Scheme Syllabus & Logbook
- G110 RYA Foiling

- G111 RYA Wing & Windsurfing
- E-G100 RYA Race Training Exercises
- YR1 RYA Racing Rules of Sailing
- YR7 RYA Handy Guide to the Racing Rules

Who Teaches What?

RYA tuition at Recognised Training Centres must comply with the appropriate tuition and safety-boat guidelines.

It is the responsibility of the Principal or Chief Instructor to ensure Instructors are teaching to RYA standards. This includes good teaching methods delivered on appropriate equipment, with suitable student/Instructor ratios, as outlined in the appropriate RYA publications.

Unless dispensation is granted by the RYA, all proficiency courses should be run with no more than six students to each Instructor.

An RYA Recognised Training Centre is required to have an RYA Senior Instructor to supervise tuition and maintain recognition for dinghy sailing, windsurfing, and wing. Further details are available within the RYA Organisation section (page 170) and included in the Guidance Notes available on www.rya.org.uk.

RYA Teaching Ratios

Instructor Qualifications	Can Teach National Scheme	Can Teach Youth Scheme	Ratio
Start Windsurfing Instructor	Start Windsurfing	Stages 1 and 2	1:6
Intermediate Instructor (Non-planing)	Intermediate (Non-planing)	Stages 1 to 3	1:6
Intermediate Instructor (Planing)	Intermediate (Planing)	Stages 1 to 4	1:6
Advanced Instructor	Advanced	Stages 1 to 4	1:6
Windfoiling Instructor	First Flights	Stages 1 to 4	1:4
Senior Instructor	Supervisory qualification		
Wingsurf Instructor	Learn to Wingsurf, Improve Your Wingsurfing	Stages 1 and 2	1:4
Wingfoil Instructor	First Flights, Sustained Flights*		
RYA Trainer Qualifications			
RYA Start Trainer	Start Windsurfing and Senior Instructor Courses	All	1:8
RYA Intermediate Trainer	Start, Intermediate, and Senior Instructor Courses	All	1:8
RYA Advanced Trainer	Start, Intermediate, Advanced, and Senior Instructor Courses	All	1:8
RYA Foiling Trainer	As a Start Trainer, plus Foiling Courses	All	1:4 (First and Sustained Flights) 1:6 (Performance Flights)
RYA Wingsurf Trainer	Wingsurf Instructor and Senior Instructor		1:6
RYA Wingfoil Trainer	Wingfoil Instructor and Senior Instructor		1:6
RYA Racing Qualifications			
Race Coach Level 1	N/A	Start Racing	
Race Coach Level 2	N/A	Start, Club, and Regional Racing	
Race Coach Level 3	N/A	Start, Club, Regional, and Championship Racing	

An Instructor who is suitably experienced and approved by the Principal or Chief Instructor.

RYA Instructor Training

The Instructor pathway in training and racing is progressive, with clear steps helping you to progress through the levels as your coaching advances and your personal skills improve. The table below outlines the qualification ladder and associated information.

RYA Instructor Qualifications	Run by	Moderator	Length of Course	Course Ratio
Assistant Instructor	Senior Instructor	N/A	Centre specific	Centre specific
Start Instructor	RYA Start Trainer or above	Moderated by a Trainer	Five days (last day is a moderation)	1:8
Intermediate Instructor	RYA Intermediate Trainer or above	None	Four days	1:8
Advanced Instructor	RYA Advanced Trainer or above	None	Five days	1:8
Foiling Instructor	RYA Foiling Trainer	None	Four days	1:8
Senior Instructor	RYA Trainer	None	Four days	Minimum of six candidates
Wingsurf Instructor	RYA Wingsurf Trainer	Moderated by a Trainer	Three days	1:6
Wingfoil Instructor	RYA Wingfoil Trainer	None	Two days	1:6
RYA Racing Qualifications				
Race Coach Level 1	RYA Trainer (by appointment) or Racing Tutor	None	Two days or assessment on a Start Instructor Course	1:8
Race Coach Level 2	Racing Tutor	None	Two days	1:6
Race Coach Level 3	RYA HQ	None	Two weekends, plus additional work	2:12

The following information provides you with a general description of each RYA windsurfing qualification, course information and content, assessments that take place, and any prerequisites needed prior to attending the course. Further information can be found on the RYA website.

RYA Assistant Instructor

This course is designed to offer an introductory level to instructing. It is for those intending to qualify as an RYA Instructor and is certified by the Principal or nominated Chief Instructor of a training centre.

Eligibility

The Assistant Instructor is a competent sailor in their chosen discipline who works under the supervision of a fully qualified Instructor at all times. Candidates must hold the minimum of an Intermediate Non-planing personal certificate or the Improve Your Wingsurfing certificate. They are not qualified to use a powerboat unless they hold the RYA Powerboat Level 2 certificate.

Training

Training is provided by the Principal or nominated Chief Instructor who holds a Senior Instructor qualification. It may be run as a specific Assistant Instructor course over about 20 hours or provided on a one-to-one basis over a longer period as on-the-job training. The Assistant Instructor (AI) qualification is centre specific; therefore the training will be related directly to the work of that particular centre.

Assessment

Candidates will be assessed on their practical teaching ability with beginners. Successful candidates will have their record card signed and be awarded an RYA Assistant Instructor certificate by their Principal.

Certificate Validity

The Assistant Instructor certificate awarded is valid for five years, at which point it is encouraged that AIs progress on to taking a full RYA Instructor qualification. Alternatively, the certificate can be reissued after the appropriate training.

Important Note

The AI does not need to hold a first aid or powerboat certificate; therefore AIs must always work with direct supervision.

The award is centre specific. Thus, if an Assistant Instructor moves from one training centre to another, the new Principal will be required to deliver centre-specific training and issue a new Assistant Instructor award.

RYA Start Windsurfing Instructor

A Start Windsurfing Instructor is a competent windsurfer trained to teach and assess the Start Windsurfing syllabus of the RYA National Windsurfing Scheme and Stages 1 and 2 of the Youth Scheme. Start Windsurfing Instructors are confident windsurfers, capable of teaching the basic skills of windsurfing in light to medium winds.

Eligibility

- Minimum age: 16
- Candidates must hold an Intermediate Non-planing personal certificate (including the beachstarting and non-planing carve gybe clinics)
- RYA Powerboat Level 2 certificate
- A valid RYA First Aid Certificate, or another acceptable first aid qualification detailed on the RYA website (https://www.rya.org.uk/training-support/Pages/first-aid.aspx)
- RYA membership
- Safe & Fun online course.

Training

Duration: Five days.

During the Start Windsurfing course a number of aspects will be covered to measure the candidate's knowledge to teach under the supervision of a Senior Instructor. Below are just some of the areas covered:

- The RYA schemes
- The Start Windsurfing teaching method (on-water, self-rescue techniques, ashore)
- Theoretical knowledge
- Shorebased-talk techniques
- Course management
- Powerboat-rescue techniques
- Personal skills and sailing assessment*
- Equipment and simulators

*During the course a sailing assessment may be carried out covering the basic skills and techniques an Instructor would be expected to show, such as stopping and starting under control, turning on the spot, tacking, and gybing. Passing this assessment is a requirement of the qualification. Further details can be found on page 28.

Assessment

The Start Windsurfing course runs over five days, with the final day moderated by an external Trainer. During the moderation candidates may be required to demonstrate confident ability in any of the following areas:

- Delivery of on and off-water sessions
- Preparation, management, and structure of the sessions
- Theoretical knowledge
- Sailing ability

RYA Intermediate Windsurfing Instructor

Role

An Intermediate Windsurfing Instructor is a confident and experienced windsurfer with wide theoretical knowledge. They are trained to teach and assess the Start and Intermediate Non-planing and/or Planing windsurfing courses of the RYA National Windsurfing Scheme and Stage 1 to 4 of the Youth Scheme under the supervision of an RYA Senior Instructor.

The Intermediate course can be assessed in two competencies: non-planing and planing. It is the first Instructor course to incorporate the Fastfwd coaching model. Candidates will cover teaching of all clinics incorporated within the Intermediate syllabus during the course.

Eligibility

- Minimum age: 16
- RYA Start Windsurfing Instructor, with evidence of 50 hours logged as a Start Windsurfing Instructor at an RYA Recognised Training Centre
- Candidates holding an Intermediate Planing personal certificate (including the beachstarting and non-planing carve gybe clinics) can qualify as an Intermediate non-planing Instructor and Stage 3
- Candidates holding an Advanced personal certificate (including waterstart and carve gybe clinics) can qualify as an Intermediate non-planing Instructor and Stage 3
- RYA Powerboat Level 2 certificate
- A valid RYA First Aid Certificate, or another acceptable first aid qualification detailed on the RYA website (https://www.rya.org.uk/training-support/Pages/first-aid.aspx)
- RYA membership

Training

Duration: Four days.

Course content:

- The RYA schemes
- Delivery of the Intermediate teaching method using Fastfwd on-water and ashore
- Self-rescue techniques
- Presentation techniques and theoretical knowledge
- The development of personal sailing skills
- Powerboat rescue techniques
- Course management
- Equipment and simulators

Assessment

There is no moderation during the Intermediate Instructor course due to candidates being continually assessed by the course Trainer. Candidates will be required to demonstrate confident ability in the following areas:

- Delivery of on-water and on-shore sessions
- Preparation, management, and structure of the sessions
- Theoretical knowledge
- Sailing ability

RYA Advanced Windsurfing Instructor

The RYA Advanced Instructor qualification is the highest Windsurfing Instructor award. An Instructor of this level is an experienced and very competent Instructor, with excellent personal sailing ability and extensive theoretical knowledge. Instructors qualified to this level are able to teach all levels of the RYA National and Youth Scheme under the supervision of an RYA Senior Instructor. The Advanced course has a clinic-based approach, appealing to a wider spectrum of windsurfers.

Eligibility

- Minimum age: 18
- Minimum personal ability of the Advanced certificate
- RYA Intermediate Planing Instructor, with evidence of 100 hours logged
- RYA Powerboat Level 2 certificate
- A valid RYA First Aid Certificate, or another acceptable first aid qualification detailed on the RYA website (https://www.rya.org.uk/training-support/Pages/first-aid.aspx)
- RYA membership

Training

Course duration: Five days.

Course content:

- The RYA Schemes
- Delivery of the Advanced teaching method using Fastfwd, on-water and ashore
- Self-rescue and powerboat rescue techniques
- Presentation techniques and theoretical knowledge
- The development of personal sailing skills
- Course management
- Equipment and simulators

On successful completion of the course, the Trainer will submit your information to the RYA Certification Department. An Instructor Certificate will be sent to you outlining the level of qualification you hold, basic terms, and the qualification expiry date.

Assessment

There is no moderation during the Advanced Instructor Course as candidates are continually assessed by the course Trainer. Candidates will be required to demonstrate confident ability in the following areas:

- Delivery of on-water and on-shore sessions
- Preparation, management, and structure of the sessions
- Theoretical knowledge
- Sailing ability

RYA Foiling Endorsement

Role

- A Foiling Instructor is an experienced Instructor with a good wind-foiling personal ability and background knowledge
- Has been trained, as a minimum, to teach the 'First Flights' course from the RYA National Windsurfing Scheme, or higher (personal foiling level dependent)

Eligibility

- Minimum age 17
- Candidates will hold the RYA Intermediate Windsurfing Instructor certificate
- Holds an RYA Sustained Flights certificate or above
- A valid RYA First Aid Certificate, or another acceptable first aid qualification detailed on the RYA website (https://www.rya.org.uk/training-support/Pages/first-aid.aspx)
- RYA membership

Training/Assessment

Four-day training course covering the following content:

- Foiling equipment: boards and foils
- Required background knowledge
- Foiling techniques
- Use of powerboats in a foiling-boat coaching environment
- Continuous assessment through the four days
- A certificate will be issued by the RYA upon successful completion

RYA Race Coach Level 1

The Race Coach Level 1 course is designed to enable Instructors to introduce relatively inexperienced sailors to entry-level racing. The Race Coach Level 1 qualification is an endorsement on an existing RYA Instructor qualification.

A Race Coach Level 1 is an Instructor who may like to get involved in setting up and running club-level competition for adults, children, and teenagers, as well as British Youth Sailing Recognised Club (BYSRC) activity. Personal competition experience is not essential, although would be an advantage.

Role

This endorsement can be obtained by Instructors who wish to teach racing skills through the Start Racing module of the RYA National and Youth Schemes.

Eligibility

It may be possible for RYA Instructors who have experience of club racing to qualify as a Race Coach Level 1 during their Instructor training course.

Alternatively, qualified Instructors may undertake further training at a later date with a Trainer.

Training/Assessment

The one-day course will include the organisation of club or inter-club racing, preparation, management of the Start Racing course, and instructional techniques afloat (at least half of the day), including the use of race-training exercises.

Assessment is continuous and on successful completion a record card will be completed by an RYA Trainer and sent to the RYA.

The course should include the following characteristics:

- An emphasis on racing as an enjoyable pastime
- Ensuring the students have a basic understanding of starting and some fundamental racing rules
- The provision of enough information for Start- or Club-standard windsurfers to compete in a club racing course safely without presenting a hazard to other sailors
- Encourage sailors to start racing and progress within the sport

RYA Race Coach Level 2 (RCL2)

A course for a competent racer with personal racing knowledge of club and/or regional racing. The aim of the course is to provide candidates with skills and techniques to coach racing to youth and adult sailors.

Role

Level 2 Race Coaches are able to deliver Start Racing at a Recognised Training Centre, and Club and Regional Racing at either a Recognised Training Centre or an Affiliated club.

Eligibility

- Appropriate racing experience (at least a competent club racer)
- Appropriate current racing knowledge (classes/pathways/Racing Rules of Sailing)
- RYA Powerboat Level 2 certificate
- A valid RYA First Aid Certificate, or another acceptable first aid qualification detailed on the RYA website (https://www.rya.org.uk/training-support/Pages/first-aid.aspx)
- Minimum age 16. Level 2 Coaches aged under 18 should be appropriately supervised by an adult who is either a Senior Instructor or a Race Coach Level 2 or above
- Previous instructing experience is preferred but is not essential if the candidate has suitable alternative experience

Training/Assessment

The RYA Race Coach Level 2 training is an intense two-day course looking at the theory of coaching and applying it through a series of practical on-the-water exercises. The focus is on how to create positive learning environments through the delivery of effective and capable coaching.

Each candidate will be expected to run a number of sessions, including providing an exercise brief, delivering on-the-water coaching with feedback, and facilitating a learning review. Assessment is continuous throughout the course.

Revalidation

Racing Coaches are requested to revalidate every five years to ensure their continued effectiveness as a coach. They need to:

- Complete the Racing Coaches Revalidation Form
- Provide a copy of a valid First Aid certificate

RYA Wingsurfing Instructor

A Wingsurfing Instructor is a competent wingsurfer trained to teach and assess the Learn to Wingsurf and Improve your Wingsurf syllabuses of the RYA National Wing Scheme. Wingsurfing Instructors are capable of teaching the basic skills of wingsurfing in light to medium winds to adults and children.

Eligibility

- Minimum age: 16
- Candidates must hold an Improve your Wingsurfing personal certificate and be able to complete a demonstration of all skills
- RYA Powerboat Level 2
- A valid RYA First Aid Certificate, or another acceptable first aid qualification detailed on the RYA website (https://www.rya.org.uk/training-support/Pages/first-aid.aspx)
- RYA membership
- Safe and fun online courses

Training

Duration: Three days.

During the Wingsurfing Instructor course several aspects will be covered to measure the candidate's knowledge to teach under the supervision of a Senior Instructor. Below are some of them:

- The RYA Schemes
- Course management
- Powerboat rescue techniques
- Personal skills and sailing assessment
- Theoretical knowledge
- Shorebased talk techniques

During the course a sailing assessment may be carried out. It would cover the basic skills and techniques an Instructor would be expected to show, such as stopping and starting under control, turning on the spot, sailing around a triangular course, tacking, and gybing. Passing the assessment is a requirement of the qualification.

Assessment

The Wingsurfing Instructor course runs over three days, with the final day moderated by an external Trainer. During the moderation, candidates may be required to demonstrate confident ability in any of the following:

- Delivery of on- and off-water sessions
- Preparation, management, and structure of the sessions
- Theoretical knowledge
- Sailing ability

RYA Wingfoiling Instructor

A Wingfoiling Instructor is a competent wingfoiler trained to teach and assess at minimum the First Flights syllabus of the RYA Wing Scheme, or higher dependent on personal foiling level. Wingfoiling Instructors are capable of teaching the basic skills of wingfoiling. During the course, candidates will be assessed on their competence to teach to the level of RYA First Flights and RYA Sustained Flights in wingfoiling.

Eligibility

- Minimum age: 17
- Candidates must hold the RYA Wingsurfing Instructor qualification
- Candidates must hold the RYA Sustained Flights personal certificate and be able to complete a demonstration of all skills
- RYA Powerboat Level 2
- A valid RYA First Aid Certificate, or another acceptable first aid qualification detailed on the RYA website (https://www.rya.org.uk/training-support/Pages/first-aid.aspx)
- RYA membership
- Safe and fun online courses

Training & Assessment

Duration: Two days.

The two-day training course covers the following content:

- Foiling equipment: boards and foils
- Foiling techniques
- Powerboat rescue techniques
- Theoretical knowledge
- Continual assessment through the two days

RYA Senior Instructor for Windsurfing or Wing

As an Instructor reading the following information you may feel you are already fulfilling the roles required of an RYA Senior Instructor (SI), or you need further knowledge and experience.

Prior to considering and attending the course it is important for an RYA Instructor who is looking to attend an SI course to understand and appreciate the varied roles an RYA Senior Instructor may play within an RYA Recognised Training Centre.

An Instructor must understand the difference in role and the importance of the SI to the RYA, their centre (or club), students, and Instructors. The following information sets out to assist in ensuring RYA Instructors understand this.

The role of an RYA SI is diverse and dependent on the individual club or centre. An SI might be a volunteer or employee, part of a small team or larger workforce, or a mixture! These circumstances will influence and dictate what type of role an SI takes on, whether they become more of a manager and role model, or remain an active Instructor.

Background Knowledge

An RYA Training Centre must have a Principal who may themselves be a Senior Instructor, or they may appoint a Senior Instructor to act as Windsurfing Chief Instructor. They would then oversee and manage the windsurfing or wing scheme delivery and ensure that tuition is organised according to RYA methods and standards.

It is the Principal of an RYA Recognised Training Centre who carries the formal responsibility for ensuring that all training complies with RYA guidelines laid down in the current Guidance Notes for inspection of RYA Recognised Training Centres.

Qualities and Abilities

An SI has a great deal of responsibility: relying on resourcefulness to solve problems as they arise, directing the work of Instructors, and assisting and supporting their team, particularly if and when they need advice. Some of the many qualities a Senior Instructor requires are:

- Soft skills: Patience, resourcefulness, having the ability to deal with students and Instructors in an appropriate manner
- Organisational: Able to ensure courses are safe, enjoyable, and informative
- Managerial: Capable of managing and supervising one or more groups ashore or afloat and ensuring each group is taught by an appropriately qualified Instructor
- Supporting and supervising: Assisting and supporting their Instructor team, particularly when they need advice and mentoring
- Knowledge of the RYA: Understanding the full requirements of RYA Training Centre Recognition and where necessary putting in place all the necessary systems and documentation. This may well include carrying out or revising a risk assessment and specifying and recording safety procedures.

Are You Ready to Be a Senior Instructor?

Apart from problems caused by deteriorating weather conditions, issues generally arise from poor planning, expectations, or a lack of communication between the SI, Instructors, and students. The SI course looks to develop, train, and assess experienced Instructors to be competent in the following areas:

- Organising and managing RYA National and Youth Scheme courses
- Organising and controlling group tuition of all ages and abilities
- Supervising, directing, and assisting a team of Instructors and Assistant Instructors

It is the Senior Instructor's task to ensure these areas all fit together harmoniously. To provide further insight, here are 10 questions an SI may receive from their Instructors. Would you feel confident in assisting them and providing them with the support and information they need?

1. One of my students is learning more quickly than the others. What can I do?
2. (On day two of a beginner's course) It's blowing force 5 out there. What do I do?
3. What can I do with my hands when I'm talking in front of the group?
4. (On the last afternoon of an Intermediate course) You've asked me in to cover for Robin while he's away. How do I know what his students have covered so far?
5. How do I tell when my students are ready to move on to the next stage of the syllabus?
6. Bob and Sally say they're too old to take part in the beachstart drill. What can I tell them?
7. What do I do if my group spreads out?
8. Why should I make sure my appearance is tidy?
9. Why should I bother with the kill cord? It only gets in the way.
10. How do I teach Jenny to windsurf? She's only got one hand.

Some of those questions should never arise, but Instructors will always look to the SI for advice.

Role

The role of an SI is challenging and rewarding, and may be the last formal course an RYA Instructor attends. As mentioned above, the most important part of the Senior Instructor's role is day-to-day organisation of each course. Every course has four elements:

1. The students
2. The Instructors
3. The fleet/teaching facilities
4. The syllabus

To enable all elements to fit together harmoniously the SI will need to consider the following:

- Daily organisation of groups afloat
- Group control ashore and afloat
- Launching procedures
- Correct teaching ratios
- Safe and effective use of safety boats and their allocation
- Correct student/Instructor matching (families etc)
- Ensuring all staff, including visiting ones, know what is expected of them
- Session planning. Before each practical session the SI must be confident each of their Instructors has a clear idea of the aim and purpose of that session so they can confirm the aims will be met during the debriefing
- An awareness of weather conditions and calling a halt to on-water activities
- Students' learning, and the content and pace of sessions
- Alternative teaching programme in the event of adverse weather (high/no wind)
- Reprogramming staff and facilities in the case of postponement
- An overall awareness of what is happening on the water among all the fleets operating in order to anticipate and help avoid potential problems
- The 'house rules' of the centre, including equipment stowage

Eligibility

Those wishing to apply for a SI course should speak to their Regional Development Officer, who will have information where courses are being run in their particular region.

Once confirmed on a course, a candidate will receive the SI Pre-work, which must be completed prior to the course, as well as any preparation set by the Course Trainer. Failure to do so may have a direct effect on the outcome.

Candidates must first be an RYA Instructor and must fulfil the following criteria before taking part in the Senior Instructor training course:

- Minimum age 18
- Two years' intermittent, or one year full time, instructing since qualifying
- RYA Safety Boat certificate
- A valid RYA First Aid Certificate, or another acceptable first aid qualification detailed on the RYA website (https://www.rya.org.uk/training-support/Pages/first-aid.aspx)
- RYA Safe & Fun online course
- Signed recommendation from either the RYA Chief Instructor or Principal, RYA Regional Development Officer or RYA-appointed Trainer
- Candidates must have personal ability to at least the standard of Intermediate

Training/Assessment

- Staffed by two RYA Windsurfing Trainers
- Courses require a minimum of six candidates
- Four days, but can be spread over two weekends, which may take longer
- SI courses may also be organised on a regional basis, actively bringing together candidates with a variety of backgrounds and instructing experience

Due to the diverse skills and knowledge an SI requires, the course covers a wide range of different, but equally as important, aspects through the following areas and delivery:

- Development of briefing and debriefing skills facilitated through a variety of tasks/sessions
- Sessions will be allocated to candidates on any part of the syllabus encouraging fresh input to candidates' skills
- Organisation and management skills
- Course planning and organisation
- A number of short on-water tasks/sessions planned, led, and debriefed by the candidates
- Shorebased teaching sessions
- Candidate-led workshops/discussions
- Training tasks led by specialist Coaches
- Continuous assessment with regular feedback after each session from the Coaches running the course
- Personal sailing and powerboat skills
- Safeguarding children and vulnerable adults
- Knowledge of centre administration and RYA inspections

Assessment

Throughout the SI course candidates will be assessed on their ability to plan, organise, and run practical sessions, as well as their input to shorebased sessions such as group discussions.

In particular, the Coaches are looking for SIs who can clearly identify and provide feedback to their Instructors on the following areas:

- Aims clearly stated (did the session have clear objectives?)
- Briefing was complete and clear (did the group know what was required?)
- Operating area identified
- The leader could be clearly identified
- The whole group was involved
- Enthusiasm was maintained
- Problems were solved
- Signals (two way) were established, including 'Abandon'
- On-water coaching took place
- Group control was maintained (no unnecessary delays) ashore and afloat
- Each student was carefully debriefed and problems discussed and solved
- Session achieved all objectives
- Students' questions were answered
- Students were informed of their successes. The follow-on session was described
- The equipment was carefully put away after the session
- Maintained good relationships with others

The course Trainers will also assess and provide feedback to the candidates regarding their knowledge and experience of the RYA scheme in order to operate as a Senior Instructor. If the Trainers are unable to confirm whether the candidates have successfully completed the course they will outline the reasons for that decision and agree a suitable action plan for future success.

Certificate Validity and Revalidation

- Senior Instructor certificates are valid for five years from date of issue when supported by a valid first aid certificate
- Certificates can be revalidated by:
    - Completing the online revalidation form
    - Providing evidence of logged teaching experience at an RYA Recognised Training Centre
    - Providing a copy of a valid first aid certificate
    - Having a valid RYA membership number
- Little or no logged experience may require a reassessment to ensure the Instructor is still up to date
- Revalidation should normally include all existing Instructor endorsements

RYA Trainer Appointment

An RYA Trainer is an experienced RYA Senior Instructor with extensive experience, who has been selected and trained as competent to train and assess Instructors. They represent the RYA and act as an ambassador for the RYA training schemes.

If you enjoy developing people's skills, are seen as a role model, and want to put something back into the scheme, then becoming a Trainer may be for you. The RYA requires Trainers with sensitivity to individuals' needs in addition to being a strong role model. Enthusiasm and a commitment to the RYA training schemes are essential, as is having an approachable and friendly attitude.

RYA Trainers need to be competent and experienced, with good teaching and coaching skills, motivational and leadership abilities, a positive and enthusiastic approach, and good communication. The role is broad and candidates must be willing to involve themselves in all aspects of the RYA National and Youth Windsurfing Schemes.

RYA Trainers are appointed by the RYA Chief Instructor on an annual basis, and are required to attend a practical reassessment every five years.

Eligibility

The RYA Trainer process is through application and selection. The RYA Chief Instructor is looking for Senior Instructors with proven ability and extensive experience of the National and Youth Schemes in their given discipline.

Qualities include:

- Displaying a confident and solid level of personal windsurfing ability
- Demonstrating enthusiasm and an in-depth knowledge of the National and Youth Windsurfing Schemes including fluency in the method ashore and afloat
- Demonstrating outstanding teaching and coaching across the spectrum of syllabi
- Motivational and leadership skills
- Good fleet management
- Positive and enthusiastic approach based on good communication skills
- Demonstrating effective communication skills, including the ability to be empathetic, approachable, and supportive for individuals and groups
- Clear ability and understanding of an effective coaching conversation and reviewing skills
- Displaying a high level of competence in the use of powerboats in a safety or coaching environment to a role-model standard

Practical competencies:

- Windsurfing – Intermediate Planing Instructor for at least three years
- Wingsurfing & Wingfoiling – Wingfoiling Instructor for at least three years

Application Process

Initial contact should be made with the relevant RYA Regional Development Officer, who can discuss the process and nominate potential candidates for consideration to the RYA Chief Instructor.

If you are based overseas you need to contact the RYA Chief Instructor directly.

It is a requirement to be an RYA member on application and for the duration of your appointment.

Selection Days

Following a successful application, candidates are invited to attend selection. The two-day selection comprises practical and theory sessions delivered to both the peer group and RYA Trainer Selection team.

The aim of the selection is to enable the selection team to form a view on a candidate's ability and experience as an RYA Senior Instructor and to assess suitability for training Windsurfing Instructors in the RYA schemes. Candidates should be able to demonstrate the qualities listed in the 'Eligibility' Section, as well as those listed below:

- Ability to organise and deliver a sharp, meaningful, and structured session, including group control
- Knowledge and demonstration of the RYA teaching method points
- Ability to organise and deliver an effective land-drill session
- Ability to review a session as an SI using an RYA reviewing method
- Ability to drive a powerboat effectively in a teaching session
- Windsurf or wing competently on a variety of equipment
- Demonstrate effective safety-boat and coach-boat skills
- Chair an effective discussion
- Show enthusiasm, motivation, and leadership

Assessment and Course Outcomes

The assessment will be based on your abilities, judged by the RYA Trainer Selection team over the two days, in the areas listed above. These will be discussed in the final debrief.

Successful candidates will be provided with development plans and invited to attend the RYA Trainers course.

RYA Trainer Course

The training course is normally run over four days and looks into the delivery of each component of an Instructor course, consolidating the skills, abilities, and knowledge required to train and assess RYA Instructors.

Assessment and Course Outcomes

Assessment is on a continual basis throughout the course, based on an overall impression of your abilities and participation, judged by the RYA Chief Instructor and the coaching team.

Candidates who successfully complete the training course will normally be provided with development plans, which will vary between individuals.

RYA Trainers wishing to become RYA Recognised Training Centre Inspectors should attend a one-day training course organised by the RYA.

Trainer Revalidation

Revalidation is on a five-yearly basis through attendance at a practical session organised by the RYA. The day includes an assessment of ability and current knowledge in the following areas to a role-model delivery:

- Techniques for teaching and assessing Instructors to current RYA teaching methods
- Peer-to-peer reviewing
- Delivery of a practical on-water session
- Personal ability
- Powerboat discipline and role-model delivery

To be considered for reappointment it is also a requirement within this five-year period for the RYA Trainer to:

- Attend at least one scheme-relevant RYA National Conference
- Run at least two full RYA Instructor courses as a Trainer
- Run at least two National or Youth Scheme courses

An update will be delivered on changes to the schemes as well as giving an opportunity to feed back to the RYA.

Instructor Training Assessment Standards

All RYA Instructors and Trainers are required to treat students and candidates with respect and fairness. They also have a duty of care.

With the nature of windsurfing and wingsurfing, and the priority of safety for all involved, it is essential that Instructor candidates be given a thorough and searching assessment. It would be dangerous to the Instructor candidate, and anyone whom they subsequently teach, if a Trainer erred on the side of leniency in awarding an Instructor certificate.

There must never be any question of relaxing the standards required for an Instructor award.

Realistic Aims

In some cases it becomes clear to the Trainer at an early stage in the assessment process that the candidate has been over-ambitious in their choice of award. In such instances the Trainer should discuss the situation with the candidate at the earliest opportunity and agree revised achievable aims.

Grounds for Appeal

A candidate has grounds for appeal if they believe:

- They have not been given a reasonable opportunity to demonstrate their competence, or
- The person carrying out the assessment has placed them under undue or unfair pressure, or
- The Trainer has reached the wrong conclusion on the basis of the outcome of the candidate's performance in the assessment

The Procedure

The candidate should first raise the concern with the Trainer to see if the matter can be amicably resolved. If it is inappropriate to consult the Trainer, or if there is no amicable solution, the candidate should appeal in writing to the appropriate RYA Chief Instructor within 20 working days of the assessment.

The letter of appeal should contain the following:

- Full details of the assessment – when, where, involving whom etc.
- The nature of the appeal
- Any supporting documentation relating to the assessment – outcome, action plans, reports etc.

On receipt of an appeal an investigative process will commence. Following investigation the candidate will be informed of the outcome, which will be one of the following:

- The original decision confirmed
- The assessment carried out again by the same or a different Trainer
- The original decision overturned and the assessment judged to be adequate

If the candidate is still unhappy about the decision they may appeal against the outcome to the RYA Training Committee.

TECHNIQUES FOR INSTRUCTING & COACHING

The main purpose of instructing or coaching is to help people learn. Therefore, any Instructor or Coach should have a clear understanding of how people learn, helping them make more effective decisions in creating a learning environment to support their students.

To be an effective Instructor and Coach we can use some helpful techniques to make the students trust us and want to learn from us. Our biggest influence is 'rapport'.

How you are perceived by others determines your credibility and therefore the influence you will have over them. First impressions are vital as it is estimated that up to 90 per cent of people's opinions of you are formed in the first 10 seconds of meeting you.

Therefore rapport = power in coaching terms.

How and Why People Learn

Understanding how and why people learn will assist our abilities and effectiveness as Instructors, helping us to understand the importance of adapting our sessions and delivery. The next section explains the different ways people absorb information and learn.

Absorbing Information

All of us see and experience the world in a variety of ways. We take in information through our senses:

- ✓ Visual – eyes
- ✓ Auditory – ears
- ✓ Reading – eyes and mental images
- ✓ Kinaesthetic – touch, feel, and movement

These senses are pathways to our brains. None of us use just one pathway exclusively – there is a significant overlap between them. You and your students are likely to have a preference:

Visual Learners

Visual preference students make up around 40–60 per cent of the population.

Students relate well to written information, pictures, and observation. Typically they will benefit from sessions where they can observe skills and possibly take notes. In some cases, information won't seem real unless they have seen it written down. They will respond well to demonstrations both ashore and afloat, and a range of visual aids.

Auditory Learners

Auditory preference students make up about 10–30 per cent of the population.

Students relate well to the spoken word. They like to hear clear, verbal explanations of skills both afloat and ashore. Often, written information will have little meaning until it has been heard, and it may help them if they read written information out loud. Auditory learners can be sophisticated speakers, and work in jobs which require this skill.

Kinaesthetic Learners

Kinaesthetic-preference learners make up around 10–30 per cent of the population.

These students learn well through touch, movement, and space, and learn skills through imitation and practise. During sessions they will like to have a go, touch, feel, and experience the skill.

Reading Learners

Will prefer to look at the relevant RYA publications. They will usually ask what topics will be covered on the next session so they can read up and investigate beforehand. Reading learners will read information to clarify and consolidate after each session. Always refer to the RYA publications to signpost where to get further information.

For further information on this area, take a look at the 'Communication Skills' section.

An Additional Learning Model

Academics Peter Honey and Alan Mumford describe learning styles in a slightly different way. However, it's important to remember there is no clear dividing line, as many people may conform to more than one style depending on what they are doing.

Active Learners – *'I'll try anything once'*

Active learners are enthusiastic and involve themselves fully in new experiences.

- They tend to act first and consider the consequences later
- They tackle problems by brainstorming and trying things out
- They become easily bored and will generally dislike activities which require them to take a passive role

Reflective Learners – *'I'd like time to think about this'*

Reflective learners like to ponder experiences and observe things from different perspectives before reaching conclusions.

- They listen to others before making their own point
- They may like to stand back and observe
- They learn by listening and sharing ideas with others
- They may prefer a slower pace and dislike taking action without having time to think

Theoretical Learners – *'How does this fit?'*

Theoretical learners make sense of skills by understanding the theory behind them and thinking through problems logically, step by step.

- They like analysis and detail
- They may ask lots of questions
- They learn best from activities which allow time to mix their observations with their theoretical knowledge
- They enjoy having books, models, and diagrams to study

Pragmatists – *'How can I apply this in practice?'*

Pragmatists think that if it works it's good.

- They are willing to try out new ideas to see if they work in practice
- They like to act quickly and confidently on ideas which attract them
- They enjoy good demonstrations
- They become impatient with long-winded explanations and discussions
- They learn best from practical sessions which allow them to test things for themselves

This information is based on the Honey & Mumford Learning Styles Questionnaire. A full version is available from www.talentlens.co.uk/product/learning-style-questionnaire.

Methods, Motivators, and Barriers to Learning

Adults and Children

Adults and children react to and learn from different styles. We need to know how to deal with both, and ensure we match styles, delivery, and also reasons for learning.

The Way Adults Learn	The Way Young People Learn
Typically more independent and self-directed	More random and Instructor/Coach led
Goal-orientated and structured approach to learning	Fun and experiential-orientated approach
Need to know why they are learning something. Want to know 'what', 'where', 'when' and 'why'. Usually need to do things for a reason.	Prefer a fun exercise or game rather than just practice
Accumulated life experience can be applied to the learning process for good and bad	May be experiencing the skill for the first time. Not biased by other experiences – free learners!
Often reluctant to get things wrong. Become frustrated when they do!	A more natural approach with fewer inhibitions. Happy to get things wrong!

Remember that everyone enjoys learning if it's fun. Make your sessions fun, inspiring, and stimulating for all.

Motivators to Learn

People are motivated by many reasons. Our awareness of this will help shape our teaching and delivery. Some examples of motivating factors are:

- Making or maintaining social relationships
- Learning to engage others – parents often learn with a view to involving the rest of their family
- A desire to achieve awards and qualifications
- Stimulation or escape from everyday life
- Interest in the subject
- Lifestyle aspiration
- Fear of failure

Barriers to Learning

If people are motivated to learn and we shape our teaching to support them, we should also be aware of the fear of failing. Some possible barriers we may encounter:

- Other responsibilities (families, careers, social commitments)
- Lack of time
- Environment – being wet and cold, or even too hot
- Feelings – looking or feeling silly
- Scheduling problems – when courses take place
- Insufficient confidence
- Inappropriate teaching methods
- Personality clashes – between student and instructor, or through lack of bonding in the group, friendships
- Being made to do the course by parent or spouse, and not interested or ready to do it

Fear

Fear is one of the main barriers a good Instructor can help students overcome. Adults and children have three principal fears when trying something for the first time:

1. **Fear of failure.** Be clear about students' progress throughout the course. Encourage them to try things out, even if it means making mistakes. If the course is being assessed, keep students informed of progress with details, and let students know the outcome as soon as possible.
2. **Fear of the unknown.** Keep students fully informed throughout each stage, and explain to them the reasons for the structure of the course.
3. **Fear of not being liked or fitting in.** Break the ice early and encourage groups to work together and get to know each other. Consider some games to help people relax.

Further Learning

A further barrier to people learning is the retention of false beliefs. For example, they believe that they can cram everything they need to learn into one short block, such as a two-day windsurfing course, expecting this to lead to a permanent change in high skill and knowledge level. It is important to reinforce how spacing their learning experiences out over time may allow them to remember and practise.

An individual's 'mindset' can be a factor, and can be a way of better understanding people's beliefs in relation to learning. People often hold beliefs that fit into one of two possible categories:

- Fixed-ability beliefs (Fixed mindset)
- Untapped-potential beliefs (Growth mindset)

Mindset is situational and dynamic. In some situations it might be more fixed than others – it can and does change.

- **Growth mindset:** Failure is an opportunity to grow. I can learn to do anything I want. Challenges help me grow. Feedback is constructive
- **Fixed mindset:** Failure is the limit of my abilities. I'm either good at it or I'm not. My abilities are unchanging. I can either do it or I can't. When I'm frustrated I give up

Ways to Break Down Barriers

- Ensure feedback reinforces the skill rather than being person orientated. For example: *'That tack worked really well because you were patient and waited for the board to turn head to wind before moving around the front of the sail'*
- Create a positive atmosphere around getting it 'wrong' – 'Have another go so we can keep making progress'
- Reinforce that we learn by doing, which is better than being told
- Be passionate and excited about having a go at a new challenge
- Encourage the concept of testing, i.e. by setting them problems to solve

By using techniques like these you will be helping your learners to create more-helpful beliefs about their learning and move away from the less-helpful beliefs they might have arrived with.

The Stages of Learning

Instructing is the delivery of new practical and theoretical techniques, usually broken down into stages where the Instructor 'tells' the students what to do and how to do it, in a 'directed' style.

Coaching implies a shift towards helping students develop those techniques into skills. It might involve more observation, feedback, and questioning to check their understanding of the technique. However, while developing skills, people will often shift between being instructed and coached.

- INSTRUCTING (Directive behaviour): *Creating the building blocks, Instructor led*
- COACHING (Supportive behaviour): *Developing the sailor's techniques, watching, asking, supporting*

You can expect your students to follow stages when learning any new technique. The skills model below provides us with understanding of where students are in their learning cycle so we can shape our teaching and reviewing styles to match.

You will need to adapt to being both Instructor and Coach. The role chosen at any time will depend on a number of factors:

- The ability and experience of the Instructor
- The type of session (practical or theory)
- The subject (a new one or developing existing skills)
- The teaching method (discussion, demonstration, or student practice)
- The environment (ashore or afloat)
- The number of students
- Where they are in the RYA scheme

A typical session might follow this simple model which shows how your role evolves from Instructor to Coach as your students progress through their course. As students progress through the stages with one technique they may begin again at the first stage with new techniques. Therefore, even experienced sailors attending advanced courses will follow the same learning process and we need to match our instructional and reviewing styles to these stages.

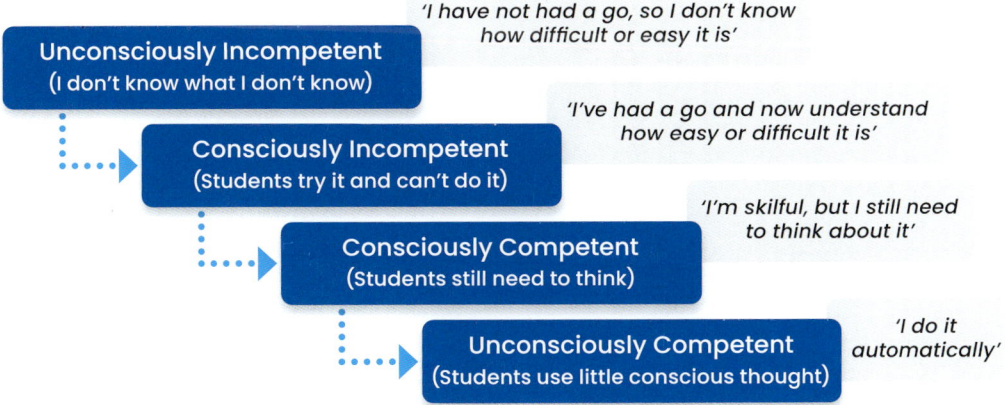

Exactly how you tackle these four stages can be determined by understanding how your students absorb information and learn new skills.

Communication Skills

As considered earlier in the 'How and Why People Learn' section, communication is more than just words. We are constantly communicating, even when we are saying nothing. Research has shown that 55 per cent of your communication is determined by your body language, posture, and eye contact, 38 per cent by your tone of voice, and only seven per cent by your actual words.

Therefore, to ensure you teach efficiently, concentrate on all these communication pathways.

Communication is a two-way process so remember you also have to listen effectively as well. The saying 'Two ears and one mouth' demonstrates the ideal ratio of an Instructor's use of words to their use of listening skills.

Effective communication can be achieved by the six 'Cs':

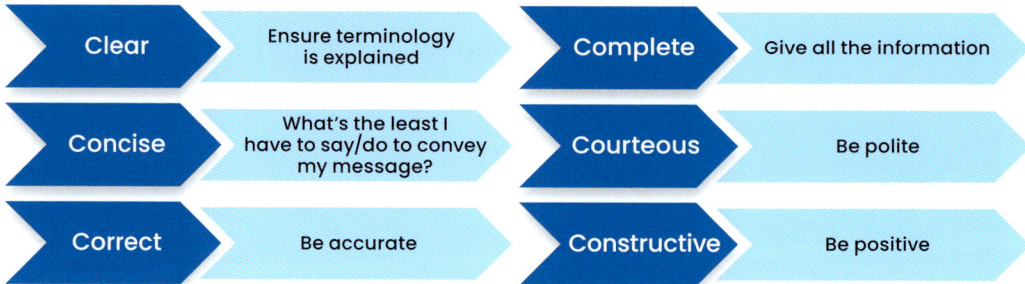

Clear	Ensure terminology is explained	Complete	Give all the information
Concise	What's the least I have to say/do to convey my message?	Courteous	Be polite
Correct	Be accurate	Constructive	Be positive

Communication while afloat is particularly important. Remember:

- Keep verbal communication to a minimum
- Project your voice towards your students and try to position yourself upwind
- Position your students where they can hear you best
- Signal students to come to you frequently for feedback and further instructions
- Use pre-agreed visual signals and agree a signal to confirm understanding

Levels of Listening

- **Cosmetic:** It looks like I'm listening but I'm not really!
- **Conversational:** I'm engaged in the conversation, talking, thinking
- **Active:** I'm very focused on what you're saying

Where possible, we need to be actively listening to our students so we really understand what they say and mean, concentrating on both the verbal and non-verbal messages they are giving.

Whatever you say, your students will typically:

- **Filter:** Pick out more or less important bits for themselves
- **Distort:** Interpret things for themselves
- **Delete:** Remove any bits that they find unclear or too difficult

It is important to check understanding often. Never assume they understand. Open questioning gets the students to think and reply, rather than giving a yes or no response. **Often less is more** – keep your messages simple and free of jargon, and back them up with demonstrations and practical examples. We will look more closely at questioning in the 'Briefing and Debriefing' section (pages 47–51).

Remember: the most ineffective question in the world is 'Do you understand?'

Non-verbal Messages

People use a variety of behaviours, such as head-nods, smiles, frowns, and laughter, to maintain a smooth flow of communication. Your students' facial expressions provide you with some feedback on the session too. The posture of the group enables you to judge their general attitude and mood. Body language and effective communication is a huge subject, so try to be your natural self.

Communication Blocks

Communication difficulties between the Instructor and the student can sometimes occur for a number of reasons:

- The student's perception of something is not the same as the Instructor's
- The student may lack the understanding of what is being taught
- The student may lack some motivation
- The Instructor may have difficulty in expressing what they want to say
- The student or Instructor has other things on their mind

Remember that Instructors are communicating all the time. Their thoughts and emotions can often 'leak' out through our verbal and non-verbal communication. Instructors and Coaches should therefore:

- Develop their verbal and non-verbal communication skills
- Ensure they provide honest feedback
- Give all students equal or appropriate attention, building rapport with every individual
- Ensure that Instructors listen to their students. Listen more, talk less!

TOP TIP

Always consider:

- **Why** you need to communicate
- **Who** you are communicating with
- **Where** and **when** the message will best be delivered
- **What** you are explaining or demonstrating
- **How** you get the information across

Being an Effective Instructor/Coach

Effective instructing and coaching needs:

- A mutual respect between the Coach and the student, with a desire to coach and be coached
- Empathy towards your students
- To inspire students
- Good communication between Coach and student – a two-way process
- A focus on clear, achievable goals
- The ability to ensure or develop the most suitable learning environment
- Truthful fault diagnosis and empathetic correction

People Skills – 'What Your Students Think of You'

Tips for gaining your students' trust:

- **Communication:** Listen to your students and respect what they tell you, working through difficult questions or situations with them. Be honest.
- **Influence:** The more you listen, the more you can influence them, build confidence, and positively reinforce
- **Rapport:** Spend time with them, enabling a rapport to develop
- **Empathy:** Express concern for and empathise with students, establish support, and identify their needs and goals
- **Preparedness:** Always set up early and be ready for their arrival
- **Appearance:** Pay attention to your personal appearance – remember the all-important first impression

What You Need to Know About Your Students

Remember that your students are going to have differing ages, genders, backgrounds, skills, hopes, fears, expectations, and aspirations. It's a good idea to gather as much information as possible on these areas from your students prior to the course. Some of this can be done on the booking form or a simple questionnaire.

Questions you might want to ask beginners:

- Why do you want to learn this activity?
- Have you done any sailing or windsurfing before, when, where etc.?
- Do you take part in any other watersports?
- Do you think you will carry on after this course?

Being prepared with this information can help you to:

- Create the right environment
- Be warm, welcoming, and friendly
- Tell them a bit about yourself
- Get them talking about themselves
- Tell them what to expect (and what not to expect)
- Create the course together
- Break the ice, making them feel relaxed and part of the group

Helping Students to Learn

Our preferred learning style will affect our teaching style as Instructors or Coaches. Therefore, we adapt our teaching style to suit these preferences, as this will create a learning environment matching all learning styles. The RYA has adopted a model which will ensure we support students' learning.

Success depends on how well you manage students from various age ranges, backgrounds, and abilities.

Examples of Models Used to Ensure Tuition Matches All Learning Styles

Find one which works for you.

IDEAS

Introduction: The Instructor explains what is to be taught and why

Demonstration: The Instructor demonstrates the skill to be taught

Explanations: Recaps the key teaching points and explains the session

Activity: Practises the skill with feedback and development from the Instructor

Summary: The Instructor summarises the skill, the lessons learned, and confirms understanding

EDICTS

E – Explanation: The Instructor gives a verbal description of the task to be taught

D – Demonstration: The Instructor demonstrates the skill to be taught

I – Imitation: The students attempt to 'copy' the technique the Instructor has just shown them

C – Correction/Coaching: The Instructor provides corrective feedback to improve student performance

T – Training/Try again: The student can apply the feedback and repeat the technique

S – Summary: Before moving on to the next exercise, the Instructor summarises the skill with the student, the lessons learned, and confirms understanding

Making the Demonstration Effective

Land drills, or on-water Instructor demonstration, introduce clarity and simplicity, and enable students to practise in a controlled environment. They are not necessarily used all the time, and can be used for students who need more development in the building of a new technique or if a technique is complicated. A land drill can work particularly well before and after a demonstration afloat to convey or reinforce the 'actual technique'.

The delivery structure for any land drill is the **WHOLE – PART – WHOLE** teaching structure. This provides a demonstration breaking down sections of a skill through:

- **WHOLE –** Demonstration (possibly silent), allowing the student to concentrate on the actions and not what the Instructor is saying. This could be done as part of the 'Whole' demonstration
- **PART –** Identifying and breaking down a particular element you want the students to concentrate on, such as hand positioning or footwork. This would be an explanation of something to consider for the 'Part' delivery
- **WHOLE –** Bring the skill/technique back together, perhaps asking the students to tell the Instructor what to do, which confirms understanding for the Instructor

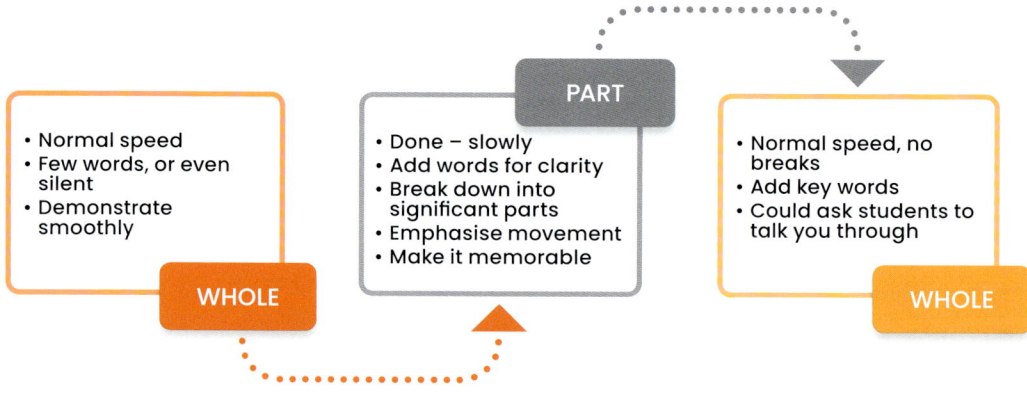

When teaching children, consider how you might be able to change the drill into a game with associated actions or use of a song etc. Land drills and simulators ashore are useful for a number of techniques where a complicated series of actions has to be co-ordinated, such as transitions like tacking or gybing. Demonstrations can be further enhanced through the use of Part-Part-Whole, breaking the skill down into easier 'bite-size' sections, depending on what you are trying to instruct, coach or achieve.

Enhancing Our Instructing and Coaching: an Insight Into Emotional Intelligence

Being emotionally intelligent is important to us as Instructors. It allows us to create rapport or empathy with our students and also enhance our effectiveness within the team. Some researchers say emotional intelligence cannot be developed or learned as it is inborn, but let's take a look at how we can try to develop our emotional intelligence as Instructors and Coaches.

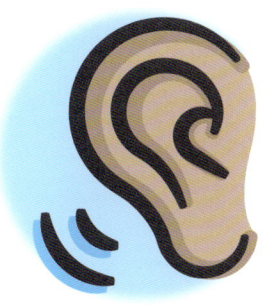

Listen

Take time to listen to what people are trying to tell you, with words (verbally), actions, and body language (non-verbally).

Body language can carry a great deal of meaning. When you sense how someone is feeling, consider the different factors that might be contributing to that emotion.

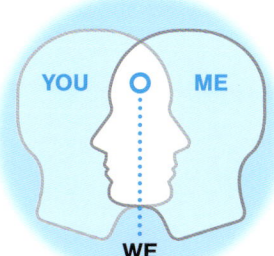

Empathise

Empathising is the ability to pick up on emotions and being able to understand another person's position. Practise empathising with other people by imagining how you would feel if you were them. Such activities can help build emotional understanding of a specific situation as well as developing stronger emotional skills in the long term.

Reflect

To reason with emotions, consider how your own influence your decisions and behaviours. When you are thinking about how other people respond, consider why they are feeling like this and how you may be able to help. Are there any unseen factors? How does your feeling differ from theirs? As you look at these questions you may find it becomes easier to understand the role emotions play in how people think and behave.

Shorebased Theory Session Skills

As Instructors, we are effectively delivering all the time, but there are also times when we need to 'provide' a talk or discussion on elements such as theory.

It is normal for people to be nervous about giving talks. Some like public speaking; others shy from it. However, with experience and practice, the nerves will start to diminish.

Words

- Clear, concise language
- If you are using technical terminology or new terms, ensure you explain
- Think before you speak
- Place emphasis on the important bits. Consider repetition to endorse/highlight an important word or sentence
- Summarise what you've said and ask questions often, especially at the end

Voice

- Vary your tone, pitch, and pace
- Speak in a conversational manner
- Build in pauses, especially at important parts
- Speak in a conversational way

Posture

Posture	Sit or stand. Try to be natural	Keep your head up. Try to breathe naturally
Hands	Uses your hands naturally if that's how you speak	Try to use your hands naturally as you speak
Movement	Moving around the group is okay as long as they can see you	Moving around the group will ensure you engage with everyone
Position	Ensure you are always in a position where all of the group can see you	
Use of notes and visual aids	Always face the audience. Stop talking while you look at your notes	It's best not to look at notes at all. Learn the presentation, and only use headings/key words in the notes
Eye contact	Ensure you make eye contact with every student often	

Good Talks Depend on Several Elements:

The Content

WHAT – Consider context and audience. Initially, look at the syllabus from the logbooks.

- What is the aim of the session?
- What are the learning outcomes?
- What do I need to teach to what level?

WHERE – Consider where this would be delivered best. Would a classroom (using whiteboard, PowerPoint, models) or outside using actual equipment be the most effective place for delivery? Also consider where YOU are most comfortable – in a classroom environment, or using models or the real thing?

HOW – Once you have the **WHAT** and **WHERE**, you need to consider **HOW** you will structure and deliver your presentation. This depends on location. However, any presentation will have:

- ✓ The beginning
- ✓ The middle
- ✓ The end

The Beginning – Tell them what you're going to tell them

The opening few moments of a presentation are very important. You want the audience to feel and think 'This is going to be stimulating and important.' Prepare an **introduction** with a clear **aim** and **outcomes**:

- What are they going to learn and why
- Whether you will be giving a handout or they should make their own notes
- Explain your structure (give headings)
- How long you will take
- How you will deal with their questions (at the time or at the end)

Some possible ways of opening are:

- Ask a question that requires a show of hands
- Begin with a quotation or tell a story
- Ask the audience to do something

The Middle – Tell them

After you have attracted your audience's attention with your introduction, move to the bulk of your presentation, or 'the middle'. Remember, attention can wander and your audience will pay most attention at the beginning and end of sections.

- Have short sections with clear headings and summaries
- Check understanding at the end of each section by asking prepared questions

The End – Tell them what you told them

- Summarise your key points
- Ask for final questions
- Link back to your beginning by revisiting the aim. What has been learnt?
- Make it significant
- Ask final questions to check understanding
- Look forwards to next session

Some possible ways of ending are:

- Issuing a challenge
- Appealing for action
- Raising a laugh and telling a final anecdote (if you are a natural joke-teller)
- Pointing to the future
- Finishing with a quotation
- Asking questions about what you've said

Handling Questions

Set the Rules for Questions

Set rules for questions at the beginning (e.g. save questions for the end, or ask questions whenever you like). Remember: when planning your talk, ensure you have sufficient time to cover everything by building in time for questions.

What to Say When You Don't Know the Answer

Honesty is the only policy when presenting to a group, and no one can know the answer to every question. It's how we deal with this situation which gives us confidence to accept there will be questions we don't know the answer to.

Compliment the Questioner

Always compliment the questioner in a sincere way. 'That's a very good question. I've never thought about it that way. Does anyone here have any ideas on that?' You might also combine this technique with 'I'll get back to you.'

The following strategies can help you field even the toughest questions with confidence.

Reflection

Repeat the question and ask your audience 'Does anyone here have any experience with that?' The audience can answer; they will love to be involved and share their knowledge.

Defer to the Expert

Sometimes a question is legitimately outside the area of expertise and there may be someone more experienced within the school or centre who you can pass it on to. You will need to decide who presents the answer – you or them. If you have used the tried and tested 'I don't know the answer but I can find out and come back to you', it is probably best for you to tell them.

Use of Visual Aids

Skillful use of visual aids can greatly enhance your presentation. Always remember that they are there to support you – they can take the attention off you periodically and allow you to think ahead. They should support what you are saying and add to the effect. Good visual aids support you, make an impact, and are memorable.

General Tips

- The best visual aid is a live example or 'real thing' of your subject matter. This enables your students to have a 'hands-on' experience, e.g. the actual equipment they will use – boat, board, sails, a buoyancy aid, a safety pack, etc.
- If the visual is comprehensive, consider giving it to your audience at the end of the lesson
- Whenever possible use pictures, diagrams, graphs, and colour
- Use visual aids to support learning, to add an impact, or to clarify a complex subject
- Models enable involvement and interaction
- Consider the use of video, white boards, and flip charts

Whichever Method You Use – Always:

Keep **I**t **S**hort and **S**imple.

Discussions

A presentation may not always be the most appropriate or desirable method, and a discussion may be considered. A discussion is a way of getting everyone to have a say about a particular subject. It is very similar to a presentation in that it has a beginning, a middle, and an end, but a chairperson is needed to manage the flow and direction. Let's explore these in turn:

Beginning – Prepare an introduction with a clear aim and outcomes. This could include:

- What are we going to discuss and what the outcome is
- How long you will take
- Stressing that everyone is allowed a voice and is able to talk

Middle – The chairperson controls the discussion by:

- Getting the entire group to talk
- Managing the group
- Developing the conversations
- Keeping the discussion on track by stopping them wandering off course. Fuelling the discussion if needed
- Managing the time
- Taking notes and steering the conversation

End – Summarise the points they have discussed.

- Link back to your beginning, by revisiting the aim and outcome
- Summarise the key points in the discussion
- Thank everyone and end the session

Styles of Discussions

There are many ways of having a discussion. Let's look at some:

- **Formal** – The chairperson leads and the discussion can be round a committee table, using a flipchart or whiteboard
- **Buzz groups** – Set the aim and send them off into small groups. The chairperson checks each group is on track
- **Informal** – Like a structured conversation. Very informal, it could be with coffee, but thoughts are recorded and used going forwards.

Briefing and Debriefing

When teaching windsurfing, your students need clear direction and input prior to going afloat, enabling them to understand and achieve the basics, as well as assisting their progression as they advance their skills.

Teaching and coaching becomes instantly easier with a good brief before the task. An effective debrief or feedback given afterwards makes for a successful session.

Creating Effective Conversations

Coaching conversations are more than simply asking questions or giving feedback. They help the learner make sense of what they just did.

If a student fails to perform a task successfully, Instructors and Coaches need to consider whether they would benefit from a coaching conversation or be better off just having another go. This may give them the opportunity to develop themselves – an equally powerful way of learning.

Conversely, if they attempt a skill but it regularly breaks down at the same point, a coaching conversation might help.

The Brief

There must be a brief *before every on-water session* and *before each new skill* is introduced. It is the most essential part to making the session effective. People should feel prepared and know what they are going to do.

A – Aim of session (What it is, why we do it)

B – Briefing, including how we do it (a demonstration may not be possible or appropriate), using visual aids/diagrams; where – sailing area etc.; when – timings, signals used, safety aspects

C – Check understanding of students (+ **coach** on the water, if possible)

D – Debrief – what happened, how can it be improved/developed?

The briefing should include:

A briefing is only good if the students understand it, so remember to check that they have. Don't fall into the trap of checking their understanding by asking the classic question 'Does everyone understand?' There will only ever be one answer: 'Yes.'

Ask questions that relate to the information that's just been given. For example:

- Where are we going to windsurf?
- What technique or task are we going to perform?
- How will you make it turn?
- Which way will we turn?
- What signal will I use to bring everyone back to the beach at the end?

If the correct answers are given, then it's likely that an efficient brief has been given. A tell-tale sign of a poor briefing is when you move away to start the task, the students get into a huddle.

The Task

Allowing students the opportunity to make and correct their mistakes before you offer support can provide a good learning opportunity. It can also help to illustrate a point, but only if appropriate.

Reviewing and Debriefing

Good instructing and coaching allows students to learn in a variety of ways and is one important element of the Instructor's toolbox. Providing effective and constructive feedback during a debrief or review will help the student understand more and maximise that learning.

- A good debrief refers back to the aim of the training and contains areas for both group and individual learning.
- Each student should be told what they did well and what they need to do to improve. There could be some generic group learning for all.
- Once you have seen the session and have thoughts/notes on performance you need to structure them to provide the group and individuals with feedback using a debriefing/reviewing model. (Support site 'CPD section' for a webinar on taking notes.)
- **Feedback**, to be most effective, should happen as soon after the event as possible. This implies it should happen on the water as the student is performing the skill, or just afterwards. If this is possible, that's where it should happen.

However, it may take place on land once the group is safely ashore, the kit has been made safe, and the students are receptive. This may mean moving to a sheltered spot, getting warmed up/cooled down, having a hot/cold drink, and 'paying a visit'.

Plan
What to do –
the brief

Do
Run the session

Review
What could be improved? How?

Ways to Provide Feedback

The RYA has chosen three feedback models as examples of review systems. These are known as the 'hairdryer', 'hamburger', and 'traffic light'. They are used in various situations to match outcome, students' needs, safety, and experience.

Rule of Threes

Providing feedback can help by reinforcing the bits of the skill that the learner performed as per the demonstration and providing a maximum of **three** key points they need to focus on again.

The critical point here is that **three** is plenty. Otherwise you run the risk of overloading the learner. However, before you give the feedback, ask yourself whether they need it, or do they just need another go?

The 'Tell' or 'Hairdryer'

There are times when we need to be clear and our instructions to be direct. Where safety is concerned, for example, we 'tell' – we are didactic in our delivery style. Another time we are direct is when students are new to the techniques and we have to tell them what to do to perform them.

What's positive about this model?

- It's quick
- The Instructor gets their point over
- Direct, specific, concentrated

What's negative about this model?

- It can feel harsh
- It can feel like a teacher at school
- It's a one-way process that omits input from the student
- Tell rather than sell

The 'Hamburger' – *Used when coaching to develop existing techniques*

When students have developed some skill in the technique and are starting to understand what they are doing or trying to do, we can shift our debrief style to being more inclusive, asking questions, and involving the student. They need a level of skill to be able to reflect on what 'good' looks like in order to reply with suitable responses to the questions about how to improve, etc.

What's positive about this model?

- It provides a framework
- It's simple to understand
- Everyone can grasp the concept at all levels
- It makes them focus on positive and negative areas

What's negative about this model?

- The Instructor may initially find it hard to create the questions until practised
- It can be weak in its directness
- Everyone is waiting for the 'But' scenario

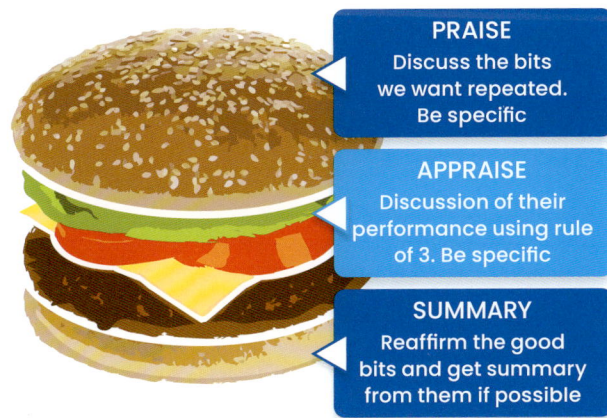

PRAISE
Discuss the bits we want repeated. Be specific

APPRAISE
Discussion of their performance using rule of 3. Be specific

SUMMARY
Reaffirm the good bits and get summary from them if possible

The 'Traffic Light' – *Used by experienced Instructors/Coaches to develop techniques*

This technique is question-based around performance. The traffic-light review opens up more opportunity for a flowing discussion. This works with experienced students; however, some may prefer a more direct approach and want to be told what's going wrong and how they put it right. This means it's back to the hairdryer! If a student invites this as a coaching solution there's no harm in accepting the invitation providing it's done with a degree of sensitivity.

However, asking questions and probing what the student thinks and feels will give you confidence that they know what they're learning and what they are trying to achieve.

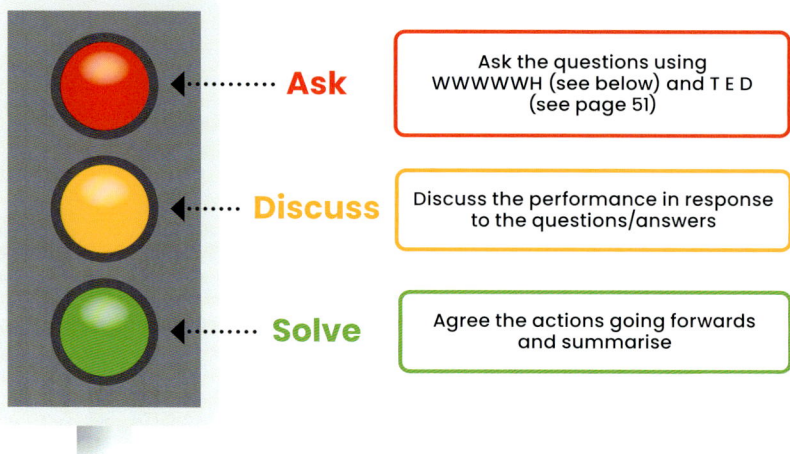

Ask — Ask the questions using WWWWWH (see below) and T E D (see page 51)

Discuss — Discuss the performance in response to the questions/answers

Solve — Agree the actions going forwards and summarise

Ask the student about aspects of their performance.

- Start with open and general questions, then focus on specific areas of performance. Listen to their response
- **Who, What, Where, When, Why, and How. Take care with 'why'**

Discuss their performance, using the response to the questions given by the student

- **What went well and what could be improved**

Solve any problems, firstly by encouraging the student to seek the solution.

- If they can't, the Instructor will do this for them. However, the student should always be the one who identifies the problem and then provides the solution with guidance and help from the Instructor, agreeing on an action plan/route towards improvement

When Are the Various Feedback Models Most Effective?

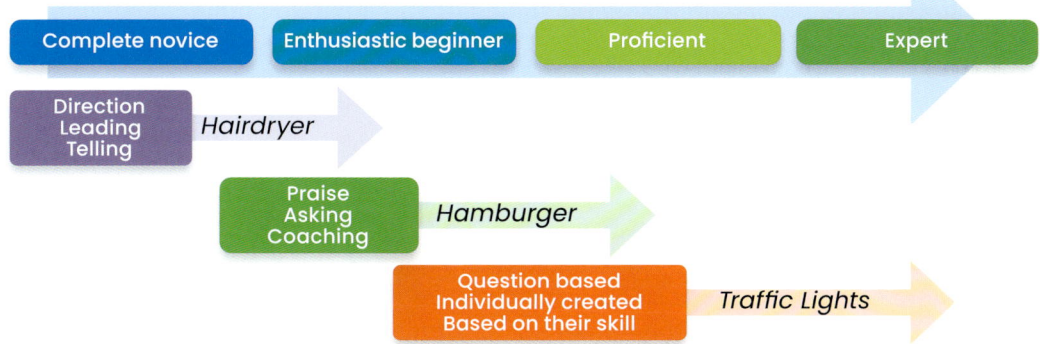

For inexperienced Instructors and Coaches, trying to create effective, question-style coaching conversations can be difficult, and many struggle to generate effective conversations even if they are proficient and have knowledge of the Who, What, Where, When, Why, and How (WWWWWH) question style.

To increase effectiveness and promote a simple, more natural questioning manner, a further technique to create an effective coaching conversation is **TED**:

- **T**ell   •   **E**xplain   •   **D**escribe

This technique will automatically force Instructors and Coaches into using one of the WWWWWH words when constructing our sentences. Starting a sentence with these three key words will make sure we lead into one of the WWWWW and H.

Here are a few example questions of **TED** being used:

TELL

- Tell me **w**hat happened
- Tell me **w**here you were looking during that move
- Tell me **w**hat order the hands and feet move in

EXPLAIN

- Explain **w**hat the customer said when they phoned
- Explain **h**ow you know when to bear away to get planing
- Explain **h**ow the sail feels in a gust

DESCRIBE

- Describe **w**hat you could try next
- Describe **w**here you should be looking during the move
- Describe **w**hat your focus is this time

By allowing the student to start analysing their performance and seeking ways of improving, they will learn how to continue this process after they have left the environment of the structured session led by an Instructor.

In effect, the Instructor is preparing the student for when the Instructor is no longer there. After this training the student should be able to continue their own progress using the skills and learning process delivered by the Instructor.

Session Planning

Planning and preparation are essential in becoming an effective instructor. A well-organised and prepared session will go a long way to minimising unpredictable occurrences!

Once you have run a few similar courses or clinics, planning will become quicker.

By identifying the aims and objectives of the session, we can identify exercises, resources available, and activities that will form the structure of a session.

Session plans should be used regardless of session length; a one-hour taster, part of a course, or when planning the different sessions of a two-day course.

They also provide a record of what has been and needs to be covered. This is useful when handing a group over to another Instructor, or may be a requirement should a question be asked regarding the content of your course or clinic.

When planning your session, ensure that you also think about the group's progression during the course. It is important to find out if there is a specific end goal, such as the group or individual looking to gain a certificate, as this will dictate the content of your plans.

There are many ways to devise or lay out a session plan, but the general content should be the same:

- Medical conditions
- Group's current ability and level of knowledge
- Learning conditions/styles
- Course type/name and date
- Timing – estimated time for each exercise. This provides approximate overall timing
- Number in group
- Session duration
- Session aim and objectives
- Equipment – type and amount, including safety provision (powerboats/radios/mobiles etc.)
- Facilities available/required
- Weather forecast (including tide, if applicable)
- Sailing area – any hazards or other water users, taking into consideration their intended location (afloat and ashore)
- Exercises, including group dynamics (pairs, individual or whole); any resources or external tools required (buoys, powerboats, whistle etc.)

Example Session Plan

Course/Clinic:	Date:	Time:	Number in Class:
Training Centre:		Length of Session:	

Aim:	
Equipment Required:	
Safety Cover:	
Radio/Mobile:	
Ability:	
Planned Learning Outcomes:	
Weather Forecast Outlook:	

Exercise	Teaching Points (To inc. any specific learning outcomes)	Group Organisation (Individual, pair, small or whole group)	Timing

Comments	
Action	

Choosing the Right Session

Choosing the right session with the right content, exercises, and challenge level can be a difficult task, especially due to the changeable environment and conditions we work in. To ensure our students continue to learn and develop we need to challenge them, and this may require us to push them outside of their comfort zone.

To do this effectively we need to understand where their comfort zone is, and how far we can actually stretch our students. Knowing our students' aspirations can help with this.

Most of our students' longer-term (as well as some shorter-term) goals and aspirations are likely to sit outside their comfort zones. With this knowledge, as well as understanding their current abilities, we can develop our students through the use of 'stepping stone' sessions, which over time meet a longer-term objective.

If we view our students' 'comfort' levels in three different stages, it's the middle stage ('Development') which will aid our students' progression:

1. **Comfort Zone**
2. **Development Zone**
3. **Out of Reach Zone**

By considering the following three areas we can shape and question the effectiveness of our session:

- **Skill:**
    - The nature of the exercise
    - How difficult or complex the skill is
    - Do they have experience in the skill they are attempting, i.e. can they already do it?
- **Environment:**
    - Impact and consideration of the wind strength, water state, and temperature
    - Are they confident in these conditions, or are they new?
- **Equipment:**
    - Is their equipment familiar?
    - Is it equipment they normally use in the current conditions?
    - Does the equipment make their new challenge easier or harder?

A Few Examples

Comfort Zone: If our students are already able to do the skill and are comfortable in the conditions and the equipment they are using, then the exercise will be within their comfort zone.

Out of Reach Zone: If the student is new to the skill and conditions, and new or less comfortable on the equipment, then we may have gone past the '**development**' stage and therefore the optimal zone for challenge and development, perhaps into the 'out of reach' stage.

A middle ground would be to introduce just one new element, a new highly challenging skill, but in comfortable conditions and on comfortable equipment.

We should usually only focus on one element at a time. For example, these could be footwork, hands, or weight, concentrating on just one of these elements at a time. This could be broken down further to include 'when to move' and 'how to move'. It's important to remember that often each of your students will be at different levels, so we may need to scale the challenge appropriately. Also, in the early stages of learning anything new, what's 'comfortable' may change very quickly, so you need to ensure we are maintaining a good level of challenge throughout a session.

TOP TIPS

- **KISS** – Keep it short and simple
- Is it a success? Instructors should test their students to see whether their session plan has translated into effective learning
- Time to learn – Instructors should make sure that their session is manageable. Don't try to cram too much into a session as students can only absorb a certain amount of information. Allow sufficient time in the session plan for the students to practise
- Learning styles – people learn in different ways, so remember it's essential to include different methods of putting something across. For further information on learning styles see pages 31–33
- Breaking down a skill into components will aid progression as it allows you to concentrate on a specific element as an example:
  - **Whole-Part-Whole** (work on the whole skill, then a specific part, before bringing the whole skill back together)
  - **Part-Part-Whole** (work on two specific but different parts of a skill and then bring it back together at the end of the exercise)

An example:

Part-Part-Whole: Improve Tack
1. **Part** – Run an exercise concentrating on the specific footwork
2. **Part** – Run an exercise concentrating specifically on vision when going through the tack
3. **Whole** – Perform the whole skill, combining the elements learnt by breaking the skill up, and see if there has been an improvement.

Group Control

Having good group control creates an effective learning environment for both students and Instructors. There are many influencing factors and, due to the teaching environment, some are easy to control while others are out of our immediate control.

What Factors Affect Our Control?

Different factors will affect different Recognised Training Centres depending on the location and courses they offer. Below are just a few of the main influences. The more experience an Instructor gains, the more likely they are to be able to adapt to or pre-empt situations, dealing with them as they occur.

The Environment

Wind, tide, and topography have an effect on how our sessions run. Strong or increasing wind often creates a more complex environment for teaching, as can a sudden decrease, especially in a tidal environment.

Stronger winds mean things happen faster. For some sessions it can be a valuable ingredient; for others it can create challenging conditions that students will find tiring.

The Task/Skill

Some skills are much easier to control than others. Exercises such as tacking and gybing can naturally keep a group close together. The addition of markers or goals to aim for will also help.

When students are learning skills, choose their equipment carefully, ensuring you consider their size, ability, the task being set, and conditions. As they progress they may require stronger winds and larger sailing areas, which are naturally harder to control.

The Student(s)

Ensure the task set is achievable in the prevailing conditions. If students start to struggle, don't hesitate in stopping the exercise, regrouping, and setting a new one that can be performed. Coming ashore between sessions and taking regular breaks provides an opportunity for feedback and/or further coaching.

Principles of Good Group Control

With experience and confidence, an Instructor is more likely to be able to keep control or 'predict' their group's chances of imploding! Below are a few considerations that will help:

Gain an Accurate Forecast

We are reliant on the conditions around us, such as wind, tide, and temperature. Gaining a forecast and outlook for the day of the course will ensure we can adjust our session accordingly. Although forecasting has advanced, it is still best to gain it on the actual day, rather than too far in advance.

Prepare a Session Plan

A well-organised and prepared session will go a long way to minimising unpredictable occurrences!

A Good, Clear Brief

See page 47.

- Aim
- Briefing
- Check understanding
- Debrief

Safety Signals: Three Basic Signals

4. Go in a certain direction – Point to direction (plus a given whistle signal), could be to go back to beach
5. Stop – Point and hold palm up to sailor (plus a given whistle signal)
6. Come to me – One hand on head (plus a given whistle signal)

GO   **STOP**   **COME TO ME**

Whistle blasts are only used to attract attention. The hand signal gives the intention/command, apart from the 'Abandon' signal

---

Communication

In addition to a clear brief, 'good communication' in general is key from the moment you greet your students, through controlling the group during sessions afloat, to presenting the final debriefs at the end of the course. Most complaints occur due to a lack of communication, but communicating clearly also assists the understanding of expectations on all parts.

Sailing Area

Choosing a sailing area that is appropriate to the group's ability and the task ahead is crucial, but remember to discuss your plans with your Senior Instructor and other Instructors at the centre.

Should there be no choice in the sailing area, you may need to increase your students' challenges by adding buoys to sail around or within.

TOP TIPS

- Students' names: Try to learn names as early as possible, making the session personable and enabling specific attention to be gained
- If covering large distances, ensure there are places to aim for, stop, and regroup
- Wait until the group has reconvened before briefing a new session or changing a current one

Successful Learning

An earlier section established how we learn most effectively, and how, by trying to solve problems and 'doing', we can work out effective solutions.

This requires the Instructor or Coach to think carefully about the aims of their session and what exercises are set. Getting the right environment for the learner is fundamental, as is choosing the skill to be learnt/taught.

What is Successful Learning?

'Successful learning is not the process of repeating a solution; it's the ability to adapt solutions to different situations. Learning might therefore be more successful when people are challenged to repeat the process of finding a solution. One requires adapting to dynamic and changing situations, whereas the other is simply reproduction.' – Bob Muir, 2016.

A Person-centred Approach

Adapting your Teaching

The GROW model encourages us to be person centred and allows an individual's preferences, aspirations, support needs, and the barriers they may face to shape what we do and when.

'Person centred' means being open minded to people's views shaping what you are doing. It is a process:

- Getting to know the person and the support needs they have
- Give people space and time to share what they think and be open minded so that their views can shape what you do
- Use the person's lived experience to shape your teaching and inform what you may need to adapt

It is a dynamic approach:

- The person knows themselves, how they communicate and learn, what they can and can't do, how they react in particular environments. You know about winging and windsurfing, the environment, equipment, and facilities
- You have different perspectives. As an Instructor, you want a plan and structure to make good decisions about a person's safety and how they can learn. The person wants to know what is on offer, what is expected of them, and how their needs will be met

Remember, it may be that a person's disability or health condition means that risks have been individually assessed, so make sure you are briefed about what your centre has put in place to support the person and enable them to participate.

Finally, being person centred means being flexible, offering the right opportunities to talk things through, avoiding the person feeling like an inconvenience where the answer is always no, and being creative in adapting your sessions.

Communication is Key

Being person centred and being a great Instructor relies on great communication:

- Talk to the person and listen to their replies
- Observe how the person communicates and interacts with others
- Ask if you are not sure
- Be patient. Give the person time to respond and participate
- Check understanding. Repeat what you think is being said
- Don't just use words. Show people how to do things and let them try
- Be respectful. Don't forget the tone of your voice and body language

Adaptations

It is important to remember that learning conditions come in many different forms. For some it's in their ability to read and write, while in others unfamiliar surroundings can cause anxiety due to uncertainty, which can lead to challenging behaviour or an individual becoming withdrawn and/or distressed. Therefore, the more we understand about an individual, the more we can adapt and in turn assist and enhance the experience we provide.

By adopting a *'Person-centred approach'*, where each individual is treated uniquely, we are able to consider how support can be provided, consider and incorporate the preferences and needs of an individual, and work with their strengths and abilities to enable them to achieve their full potential. Here is how we can achieve this 'Person-centred approach':

- **Communicate with the individual:** Ask them what their likes and dislikes are, what are their preferred communication styles, which situations might make them feel anxious or scared
- **Be empathetic:** Have an appreciation of the individual's needs and abilities in terms of social interaction and activities. Empower them to make their own decisions
- **Take an active interest in the person themselves:** This will enable you to learn about and work with them on their preferences
- **Create learning environments:** Structure and routine often assist many individuals through predictability and making the world feel like a safer, more accessible place. Therefore, knowledge of timings, as well as what is happening when, is important, as is sticking to those plans. Creating this environment will enable individuals to feel calmer while learning
- **Consider a 'Transitional Booklet':** This could be a great resource to introduce to your centre. It won't be required by everyone, but it will enable groups to talk and gain understanding about what they are going to do for those who will benefit. The booklet can talk about who they are going to meet, their names and what they look like, the centre, and what the centre looks like and the facilities (entrance, reception, changing rooms, toilets etc.). It can also describe what is involved in going afloat, the boats, safety boats, and the sailing area. A video version could also make a great resource for individuals or groups to watch prior to their visit, or recap afterwards
- **Enhance booking forms:** Consider adding a general statement for learning conditions, enabling the participant/parent(s) to provide information and complete if they wish
- **Break down activities and skills:** Use a 'step by step' approach. Repeating words or images will aid reinforcement and learning. Additionally, you could organise a number of days which slowly build on progression towards getting afloat:
  a. Invite the group/individual to take a look at the centre and walk round, feeling the wetsuits and touching the boards and rigs.
  b. Encourage them to climb onto the board when it is ashore, try on a wetsuit up to their knees or wherever they feel comfortable etc.Remember, *everyone* has a preferred learning style, generally a combination of a few,

namely visual, auditory and/or kinaesthetic. It is therefore important to use a combination of visual, auditory, and kinaesthetic messaging to reinforce communication or instructions being given. These might include the written word, symbols and pictures, sign language, or electronic devices.

The need to wear specific clothing, or indeed the need for a change of clothing in a sailing environment, may be a consideration for some individuals. The ability to ease students into the environment in which they will be learning through short visits, the opportunity to walk around in advance of the course, or perhaps even visiting the venue for a picnic, will go a long way towards setting them up for a successful and enjoyable experience.

Other adaptations may include changing the scope of sessions. For example, keelboats, which are more stable and where wetsuits are not required, might be more suitable, whereas for others this may not be a problem.

Assessing Abilities

All the RYA-certified schemes are based around a competence-based ability. Students are awarded the certificate based on their performance and practical knowledge. Therefore, the syllabi set out criteria for assessment to assist the Instructors. The types of student assessment are:

- **CAN** – They demonstrate the technique, albeit they may not be competent and skilful
- **UNDERSTANDS** – They affirm by question and answer that they know what they are expected to do, but again they may not be competent or skilful
- **KNOWLEDGE OF** – Students are not tested. Instructors deliver the session/theory topic etc. and there is no expectation or assessment of skill

As the course progresses the Instructor will be carefully monitoring students' progress to see if the pace is too fast, too slow, or just right to be challenging, informative, and achievable.

Finally, at the end of the course, the Instructor or Coach has to decide, with the help of the Chief Instructor or Senior Instructor, whether or not the objectives of the training have been achieved.

Ultimately, the question may be whether or not to award the certificate. Never forget that most people are doing this for fun, and recognising the progress that your students have made through the award of certificates is more likely to motivate them to continue than withholding the certificate because they cannot perform the task every time!

Assistance Required to Complete the Course

The 'Assistance required to complete the course' line of the course-completion certificate should be treated with care. Only list a disability if it directly affects the holder's ability to handle the equipment, so the prosthesis that gives a user complete function is of no consequence. However, a visually impaired person may have the endorsement 'Requires visual assistance on the water'.

Certificates

RYA certificates provide a great incentive to continue training, giving a clear measure of an individual's progress. Certificates are signed by the Chief Instructor and/or Principal of the centre.

The Chief Instructor will advise on the importance of keeping students (and their parents, if children) informed of their progress through the course, and what students can realistically achieve by the end. It is important we manage their expectations as they progress. This could involve telling one of the students that they may not achieve the required standard laid down in the syllabus. The Instructor should highlight what can be achieved and agree with the student on how to get the best-possible value from the course. The Instructor is typically supported by the Chief Instructor when dealing with parents of children.

A lack of communication between Instructor and student is one of the most common reasons for complaints about RYA courses.

Summary

To ensure inclusivity and increase the effective support we provide our students, we should aim to:

- Remember no two individuals are the same
- Create rapport, be empathetic, and develop our verbal and non-verbal communication
- Engage early with the support network and make specific, bespoke allowances, and ensure you understand their particular unique requirements/needs
- Consider bespoke sessions to create unique environments linked to their preferred learning styles, taking breaks from the programme
- Consider what pre-course guidance, specific resources, and assistance you may be able to provide
- Be conscious of any literal communication and language use
- Check out the many resources available to help, such as RYA Sailability; the National Autistic Society website, and other RYA Recognised Training Centres who may be able to provide guidance

Further Resources

Sailability – https://www.rya.org.uk/club-centre-support/affiliates/sailability-club-and-centre-support/disability-awareness

Equality, Diversity, and Inclusion – https://www.rya.org.uk/about-us/policies/equality-diversity-and-inclusions

TEACHING THE RYA WINDSURFING SCHEMES

Introduction

The following section provides suggested teaching aids and session plans for the delivery of the RYA National and Youth Windsurfing Schemes.

Planning and preparation are essential to becoming an effective Instructor. Understanding how to put together a successful, well-timed session plan with useful aims, objectives, and exercises that break down individual techniques are just a few of the areas covered in this section.

The teaching aids and session plans within this section should be used as a reference and guide, backed up by a combination of information gained during your Instructor course, relevant RYA publications, online information, and most importantly a large dose of Instructor's enthusiasm!

RYA National Windsurfing Scheme

The RYA National Windsurfing Scheme is about teaching students techniques that will help them throughout their windsurfing career. It is also the basis on which the personal sailing requirements are set for RYA Windsurfing Instructor qualifications. See pages 12–28 for further information.

The RYA Windsurfing Schemes provide an easy and accessible way to progress in windsurfing, with certificated courses and ways to log progression. RYA publications W1 RYA Youth Windsurfing Scheme Syllabus & Logbook and G47 RYA National Windsurfing Scheme Syllabus & Logbook provide a comprehensive syllabus and log for practical and theoretical content covered during an RYA course.

The scheme exists to promote windsurfing in an enjoyable, safe, and informative manner, providing people with the techniques and confidence they need to pursue the sport. It is important that students enjoy their time afloat and improve their techniques.

By the end of the course, students should have achieved a practical understanding typically using the correct techniques, but their manoeuvres will not always be successful or skilful. However, such a student may still be awarded a certificate.

Relevant Publications
- W4a Start Windsurfing Teaching Method
- W1 RYA Youth Windsurfing Scheme Syllabus & Logbook
- G47 RYA National Windsurfing Scheme Syllabus & Logbook
- G111 RYA Wing & Windsurfing
- G110 RYA Foiling

Additional RYA publications will also prove useful by increasing and improving Instructor knowledge and expanding on the theory taught throughout the scheme.

Courses Within the National Windsurfing Scheme

Introductory Session: *Taster*

One of the best opportunities for introducing children and adults to windsurfing is the taster session. Every year thousands get their first taste of a sport through this.

The taster is most commonly delivered as either a one- or two-hour session, and it is important that Instructors teaching the Youth Scheme have a basic understanding of how children learn and what equipment is suitable.

As a guide, in a two-hour session you should aim to get a group of six starting with fun games and introductory sessions before progressing onto the water with the sailing position and turning around. The aim remains having fun while giving them the buzz.

Start Windsurfing

As students need no previous experience, the Start Windsurfing course is designed to teach the basics of windsurfing using the Start Windsurfing teaching method, W4a, found on the RYA Training Support Site Document Finder. After the course, students should be able to sail to a chosen point on the water and return to where they started in light winds.

Intermediate Windsurfing

Prior to starting an Intermediate Windsurfing course, it is important that students either hold the Start Windsurfing certificate or are of that ability using all points of sailing in light winds.

The Intermediate course is split into the non-planing and planing courses. It should develop the student's current techniques and improve their stance and ability to get the board going. The exhilaration of speed and their improved theory knowledge will develop a relaxed blasting in the harness and/or the footstraps. Beachstarting and the non-planing carve gybe can be taught as separate clinics, or as part of the course.

Advanced Windsurfing

Once the Intermediate Windsurfing course, or Stage 4 of the Youth Scheme, has been completed, or when a student is comfortable in footstraps and harness in planing conditions, they should be ready to move on to the Advanced Windsurfing course of the National Scheme.

By the end of the Advanced course, students should have improved blasting control to aid early planing and be able to tack on a variety of boards in varying conditions. Additional clinics will help them master the waterstart and the infamous planing gybe.

RYA Foiling Courses

The RYA Foiling courses are available in both the National Sailing and Windsurfing Schemes. Having completed Intermediate Planing Windsurfing, and once a student is comfortable in their harness and footstraps, they would be at a good level to progress on to the Foiling courses.

The courses have been designed to progress students from their first foiling takeoff to sustaining flights and entering the world of foiling transitions.

With a range of courses available, First Flights introduces the concept of foiling, equipment, basic knowledge, and first takeoffs. Sustained Flights builds confidence and technique to sustain flight, with Performance Flights tackling teaching the techniques required to sail in a range of conditions and foiling into tacks and gybes.

Youth Windsurfing

The RYA Youth Windsurfing scheme is designed to be an easy and accessible way to teach kids and get them up and windsurfing as quickly as possible.

Run over a number of short sessions or full days, the syllabus of each stage is broken down into easily achievable bite-size chunks, helping children progress, have fun, and enjoy the sport.

Stage 1 provides an introduction to the basics of getting on the water, windsurfing across the wind through fun games and exercises.

Stage 2 develops the basic skills learnt at Stage 1, enabling sailors to go further afield, sailing up and downwind, tacking and gybing. This is the equivalent to Start Windsurfing.

By Stage 3, youth windsurfers will have an improved stance and confidence helping them sail in a wider variety of conditions, windsurfing on all points of sail, and learning the skills to use the harness. This is the equivalent to Intermediate Non-planing.

Stage 4 is all about the footstraps, increasing confidence, and blasting around prior to progressing on to the Advanced clinics of the National Windsurfing Scheme. This is the equivalent to Intermediate Planing.

Remember

The RYA produces a free taster-session certificate, so everyone can go home showing what they have achieved and where they can do more.

By getting the taster sessions right the courses will fill themselves, ensuring you always enthuse potential clients, and they see windsurfing as fun.

The Youth Scheme should be taught using the same Start Windsurfing teaching method, but adaptations in the use of the method are required.

For knowledge and information on the background theory and the different approach to teaching people, refer to the 'Techniques for Instructing & Coaching' section.

THE RYA WINDSURFING COACHING SYSTEMS

Technique expert Simon Bornhoft worked with RYA Training to provide the Windsurfing Scheme with a simple coaching model. This model focuses on the exact techniques required to make a real difference on the water.

For the Instructor, in reality 99 per cent of people who start windsurfing want to learn so they can blast up and down and turn around quickly. Effective coaching therefore addresses the end user's focus by getting students on the water quickly and into the thrill of the sport.

As any good Instructor knows, a student's success can often come down to one very small basic point that makes all the difference.

For the student, the coaching guide also acts as a self-reminder system by concentrating on cultivating the techniques which are an integral part of progression and are transferable into every area of the sport. The model is embedded from the Intermediate Windsurfing course and upwards, but a basic form can be used during Start Windsurfing tuition.

The model is simple, memorable, and incredibly versatile. There are five key elements which are supported by some very specific actions and techniques. It is best to concentrate on one or two specific points at a time and use them as a student and Instructor prompt while teaching.

The five key elements:

Vision • Trim • (Counter) Balance • Power • Stance

VISION – Maintains our Sailing Line
Where we look, our sailing line, and how we use our head are always the first considerations before any other action. Vision is a good starting place for our coaching.

TRIM – Keeps the Board Flat
A flat board is a fast and stable platform which increases the ease with which we can control the board and rig in any situation. All the actions we coach should refer back to trim.

BALANCE – Forms our Framework
Balance, or 'counterbalance', refers to our continuous objective of maintaining our distance from the rig (by extending the front arm) and always opposing and counterbalancing the rig's pull, position, and movement with our body.

POWER – Channels the Rig's Forces
Power refers to channelling the rig's forces by sheeting the boom in, back, and down, in order to help keep the board flat. Critical in many techniques learnt in windsurfing.

STANCE – How we use our Body
Stance refers to how we position, angle, and direct the rig's forces with our body. As Instructors, we can recommend some very specific actions to create a range of movement that maximises the effect of our body in a changing windsurfing environment.

Teaching the Youth Windsurfing Scheme

The RYA Youth Windsurfing Scheme combines training and racing into one logbook, providing a clear progression. In bite-size chunks, it takes beginners from scratch to hooking in and hanging on in no time. Each course builds on individual techniques and confidence along the way.

The syllabus for youth windsurfers is set out in stages and clearly expressed in terms of 'competencies'. As the student is able to do each technique, it can be signed off. When all the techniques in a particular stage are completed, the certificate may be issued. On any course it is possible that some students will complete some extra techniques from the next stage, in which case those techniques can also be signed off. Remember to use the 'Try Something Different' section in the logbook too!

Students can record their achievements up to Stage 4, when they will have the techniques and ability to progress on to the Advanced Windsurfing course and clinics.

Throughout Stages 1 to 4, there are 'Take a Challenge' elements. These are not part of the main certificate but are fun things for the group to try and get signed off.

Good Old-fashioned Fun!

Fun is fuelled by enthusiasm, especially when it's pouring with rain and freezing cold. Fun is how kids will remember the course and the techniques covered. Getting wet with the group and being in with the latest craze, TV programme, or film will bring all kinds of fun options to the sessions.

A group of eight-year-olds will be very different to teach compared to a group of 14-year-olds, so ensure the session is pitched at the right level. Although they are following the same scheme, being adaptable is crucial.

Equipment

One of the most important factors to get right when teaching children is the equipment. If we get this wrong, it has the potential to put them off for life. Remember that small equipment does not mean it's been designed for juniors, and advances in equipment have made teaching more accessible. Negative experiences, and watching children struggle to pull their sails up with the boom set way overhead, should be a thing of the past.

As children progress through the Youth Scheme, it is important to move towards sails which can be tuned. Ask yourself *'Would I dream of going out in planing conditions using a training sail with harness lines on?'* Hopefully the answer is NO!

Budget restrictions in a centre can limit the equipment. However, it is important to encourage young prodigies to stick with the sport. Most manufacturers have an affordable and impressive range of boards and sails, covering everything from the first experience to chosen disciplines such as racing, freeride, and freestyle.

If budgets are a problem, there are a range of options and adaptations which enable children to learn about the equipment and the wind in an enjoyable environment. If adult equipment is your only option, ensure it is adapted to teach children. Here are a few suggestions:

Rigging sticks: A rectangular piece of material and two sticks. Cheap, easy to make and incredibly effective for that initial experience or a strong-wind alternative. They are easy to use, fun for all, and a great way to introduce wind awareness and the basics of how a board works.

Setup: If the centre invests money to provide correct equipment it must be set up properly. So, think basics: the centre of effort must be able to reach behind the daggerboard/centre of lateral resistance to ensure it has directional stability. Match the right boards with the right rigs.

Boards: Children who are small enough to use a 2.5m rig don't need the volume of an adult beginner board (219L). Try to use something smaller, such as a board the centre may be currently using for their Intermediate adult courses (175L or 150L). Unless designed specifically for kids, most fins supplied with beginner/intermediate boards will create too much resistance due to their length, in relation to a super-light children's rig.

Most introductory and progression boards are, or can be, supplied with plastic fins. If not, a few cheap second-hand fins can be adapted and kept in reserve for your children's courses. Try cutting these cheap fins in half.

The correct equipment is just one of the essentials. Tuition should also be adapted, providing a safe, hands-on experience in a fun environment.

Safety Considerations

When working with juniors, always consider Instructor responsibilities, Safeguarding considerations, and practical challenges such as the increased heat loss in children compared to adults. Devoting time during staff training to develop activities on and off the water to support the Youth Scheme may be crucial to successful youth participation at the centre.

Keeping Them in the Sport

The RYA is continually working towards increasing initial experiences and ongoing participation through the Youth Scheme and initiatives such as OnBoard. For further information on current RYA initiatives, check out the RYA website.

Teaching Start Windsurfing (W4A)

Introduction

The RYA has developed a basic teaching method that introduces people to the sport in a quick and easy way. The content of this basic teaching system is mainly for Start Windsurfing and as a guide for teaching Youth Stages 1 and 2. The guide (W4a) is clearly split into sections and described in session plans for ease of use and understanding by both the Instructor and the student.

When teaching children, Instructors will need to adapt the delivery of the method to be more appropriate, especially in the amount taught in one session and instructional method.

Each session plan should consider the content of the course's syllabus from within G47 RYA National Windsurfing Scheme Syllabus & Logbook and W1 RYA Youth Windsurfing Scheme Syllabus & Logbook, but most importantly contain a good dose of Instructor's enthusiasm and adaptations to the environment they are teaching in!

Evaluating Your Students' Ability

The Instructor needs to have covered all areas of the syllabus outlined in G47 RYA National Windsurfing Scheme Syllabus & Logbook or W1 RYA Youth Windsurfing Scheme Syllabus & Logbook to ensure students can be awarded a Start Windsurfing and Youth Stage 1 certificate. There are many ways to assess a student to see whether they understand or can perform each area of the syllabus. For example, a triangular course or follow my leader may be the easiest option to assess their ability to tack, gybe, and sail on all points, but there are lots of alternatives. Get creative and have fun with the group.

Definitions Used During the Teaching Method

- **Aim:** The purpose of the session and what you are trying to achieve
- **Session consideration:** The procedure the Instructor follows. Key teaching points may be underlined
- **Teaching sequence:** The order of delivery
- **Teaching points:** Key, simplified points that help to make a technique achievable

The method is split into two main sections – 'onshore' and 'on-water'. Any theory or knowledge should be taught practically wherever possible to maximise enjoyment and time afloat. The onshore sections should be taught using a basic simulator, enabling the students to get to grips with new manoeuvres prior to heading out onto the water.

Land Drills

Land drills introduce clarity and simplicity, and they enable students to practise in a controlled environment. They are fundamental to the learning process for students and do not necessarily have to be used all the time.

When teaching children, demonstrations can be provided on the simulator, but children must not be placed on the simulator.

Providing a Simulator Demonstration

To help provide an effective and meaningful demonstration, the following model can assist simulator demonstration. It has four distinct stages:

1. Introduction: Introduce the task, the reason for doing it, and how it fits into the overall programme.
2. Demonstration: Instructor demonstrates using simple, uncomplicated language.
3. Student attempt: Each student attempts each manoeuvre and corrective feedback is provided by the Instructor, who uses each student to emphasise important teaching points.
4. Summary: Off the simulator, the Instructor provides a final summary of what has been achieved and how it fits in the overall programme.

Choosing the Right Simulator

A windsurfing simulator is a requirement of RYA recognition and one of the many aids available when teaching windsurfing. If used well, it can be very effective for the initial introduction and for further coaching at all levels.

Basic Simulators

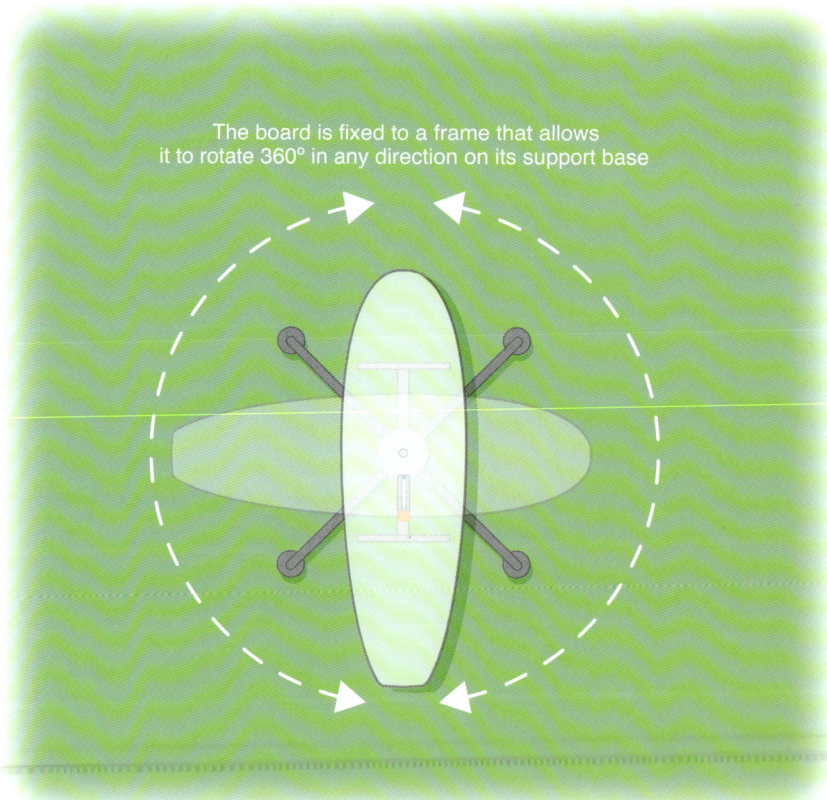

The board is fixed to a frame that allows it to rotate 360° in any direction on its support base

Used for teaching RYA Start Windsurfing, basic simulators should preferably have the following characteristics:

- Low to the ground
- Stable base
- Solid assembly
- Damping system
- Realistic board
- Suitable rig
- Mobility (if you need to move it)
- Clear wind location
- Sufficient space around it

THE START WINDSURFING TEACHING METHOD

Onshore One (Delivery Ashore)

Instructor demonstrations delivered ashore on a simulator through a briefing and demonstration. Each stage may break this down even further to aid learning, dependent on group level and environment.

1. Introduction to kit.
2. Getting started: secure position, static turn, sailing position, followed by on-water practice and consolidation.
3. Steering the board.
4. Tacking.
5. Safety.

On-water One (Delivery Afloat)

Aim: Various short sessions encouraging students to achieve goals and learn progressively, incorporating Instructor demonstrations and students sailing across the wind.

Once students have a reasonable grasp of sailing across the wind, they should proceed to Onshore Two.

Students should be issued with the relevant clothing, told how to wear it, and have the importance of doing up buoyancy aids and wetsuits explained before heading out onto the water.

Session Structure

- Instructor to recap session
- Teaching aids: Instructor equipment, buoys, powered craft
- Laying an across-wind course can aid group control
- A safety boat should always be afloat and ready to use
- On-water One should be delivered as a number of short sessions, mixed in with simulator sessions, encouraging students to achieve goals and learn progressively
- Make sure students' goals are visible, such as the use of marker buoys
- Before going afloat, the Instructor should provide the students with a brief including sailing area, safety signals, and any hazards

Teaching Sequence

Instructor demonstrates sequences afloat in sections:

1. Sailing across the wind:
   a. Secure position.
   b. Static turn.
   c. Sailing position.
2. Steering.
3. Sailing across the wind with a tack.
4. Session Seven (safety) can be talked about before going afloat or during a break in the sailing lesson.

Onshore Two (Delivery Ashore)

1. Recap Onshore One.
2. Upwind sailing.
3. Downwind and gybing.

On-water Two (Delivery Afloat)

Aim: Incorporating various sessions to introduce these elements progressively:

1. Upwind sailing.
2. Downwind and gybing.
3. Sail Safe.

The two sections (upwind and downwind) of Onshore Two may be split, depending on conditions and the group's ability.

All teaching demonstration for Start Windsurfing, Onshore One, and Onshore Two should be utilising a beginner's simulator with board and rig.

Sail Safe should be covered during the course, but fully recapped as the seven common senses before completion.

The Start Windsurfing Method

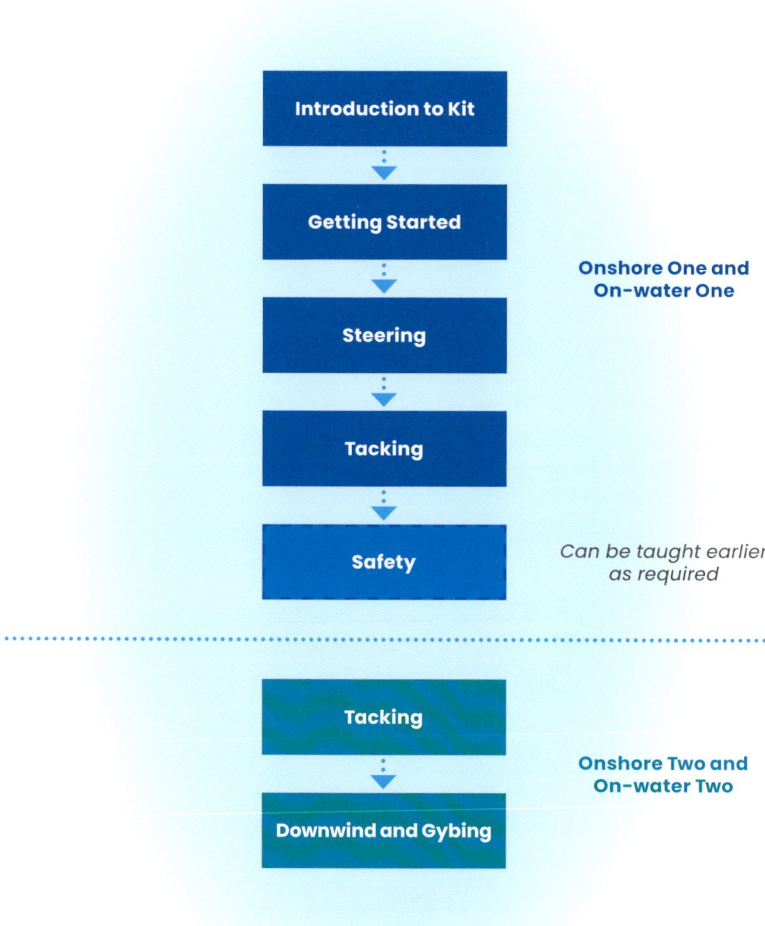

Introduction to Kit

↓

Getting Started

↓

Steering

↓

Tacking

↓

Safety

Onshore One and On-water One

Can be taught earlier as required

Tacking

↓

Downwind and Gybing

Onshore Two and On-water Two

Session 1: Onshore One – Introduction to Kit, Including Personal Clothing

Aim

A brief introduction to the course, the function of various components of the board and rig and, if appropriate, demonstration of rigging or basic tuning techniques.

Session Considerations

- Instructor brief and introduction
- Introduction of personal clothing and issuing of relevant clothing
    - Wetsuits and buoyancy aids
    - Importance of correct fitting and 'doing up' buoyancy aids
- Utilise a student's board with the rig (de-rigged, or in whatever state the students will find their own)
- The board and rig used for the demonstration must be identical to that used by the students
- Use the proper terms for each item and keep technical jargon to a minimum
- Cover the function of each component
- Demonstrate how the equipment is rigged and made ready to sail
- Ensure the process is simple. This is best done in stages, with the Instructor showing a small part, then the students copying with their rigs, and returning to the Instructor for the next stage

During the Instructor's rigging demonstration, the students should gain as much hands-on experience as possible.

Teaching Sequence

The board:

1. The front (nose), back (tail), top, and bottom.
2. Fin and daggerboard/centreboard operation.
3. Mastfoot fitting and towing eye.
4. Centreline.

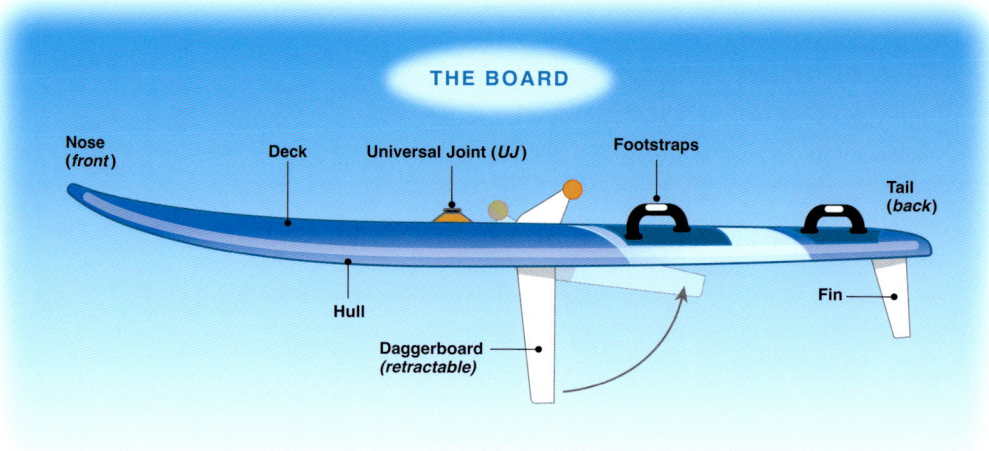

The rig:

1. The mast, boom, sail, mastfoot, and uphaul.
2. Slide sail onto mast and attach mastfoot.
3. Check boom height (chest).
4. Tensioning of the sail (downhaul and outhaul).

Teaching Points

- Wind awareness
- Connecting board and rig together
- Picking up the rig and carrying it
- Storing the rig

Session 2: Onshore One – Getting Started – Secure Position

Aim

To teach the student how to climb onto the board, pull the rig out of the water, and get into and maintain the secure position.

Session Considerations

- Instructor to provide a clear demonstration ashore to help build a progressive sequence
- Utilise a beginner's simulator with board and rig
- It is important that when the students are on the simulator, they understand why and how the board must be manoeuvred and held in the secure position
- After the Instructor demonstration, encourage candidates onto the simulator to ensure they understand the importance of key positions and actions by copying the Instructor themselves

Teaching Sequence

1. Approach the board from the <u>opposite side to the rig, wind coming from behind the sailor.</u>
2. Place hands <u>either side of the mastfoot, climb on, place knees on the board, and keep weight over the centreline.</u>
3. Grab hold of the <u>uphaul</u> and check where the <u>wind</u> is coming from.
4. Keep hold of the uphaul and <u>stand up</u>, keeping <u>feet comfortably either side of the mastfoot on the centreline.</u>
5. With <u>straight arms</u>, <u>lean back</u> slightly to break the seal of the sail on the water, and allow the water to drain away.
6. Keeping the legs flexed, work hand over hand up the uphaul, eventually holding the mast <u>below the boom with extended arms</u>.

5.

7. <u>By leaning the rig either backwards or forwards (if necessary), position it at 90 degrees to the board</u> to find the <u>secure position</u>.

7.

Coaching Points

- Weight on <u>centreline</u>
- Take time over the uphaul process to drain water off rig and keep back straight
- <u>Keep arms extended</u>
- The Instructor will need to show an upwind rig recovery when afloat
- The final position should be relaxed with flexed legs (a <u>V shape between body and rig</u>)

Session 3: Onshore One – Getting Started – Static Turn

Aim

Delivered on a simulator, demonstrating how to turn the board through 180 degrees, either towards or away from the wind, and once complete return to the secure position.

Session Considerations

- Instructor to demonstrate the steering sequence <u>once in each direction</u>
- Then add the teaching points on the <u>second</u> demonstration
- Students should be encouraged to give feedback as a means of checking understanding
- This demonstration can be altered and used to show a turn away from the wind if required
- Some students will find a turn away from the wind easier at first
- The Instructor should be confident that their teaching environment is suitable and take into consideration downwind drift

Teaching Sequence

From secure position:

1. <u>Lean the rig</u> towards the <u>back of the board</u>.

1.

2. As the front of the board turns towards the wind, <u>take small steps</u> around the front of the mastfoot.
3. <u>Keeping the rig inclined</u>, move the sail across the back of the board.
4. Having turned the board through 180 degrees, resume the new secure position.

2.

Coaching Points

- Importance of taking <u>small steps</u>
- Allow the board time to turn <u>by moving the sail slowly</u>
- The <u>lower</u> the rig is leaned towards the back of the board, the faster the board will turn
- After each turn, ensure feet and body are correctly repositioned in the secure position

Having covered the 'Static Turn' onshore, it is a good time to head afloat and practice, prior to moving on to the Sailing Position.

Possible exercises might include (See Session 5 for full details) static turning – either up/downwind or both:

a) Students to experiment how leaning the rig turns the board slower or faster.
b) This can be done in both directions and could be developed into a challenge to see how many static turns they could do in a set amount of time.

If required, this demonstration can be altered and used to show a turn away from the wind, which some students may find easier at first.

Session 4: Onshore One – Getting Started – Sailing Position

Aim

Delivered on a simulator, demonstrating how to get into the sailing position.

Session Considerations

- Instructor to provide <u>two demonstrations</u>:
  - <u>Show all the actions</u>
  - The second demonstration should show steps 3, 4a, and 4b as a flowing movement with specific coaching points brought out

Teaching Sequence

From secure position:

1. Identify a <u>goal point</u> across the wind, in line with the front of the board.
2. Take your <u>front hand</u> off the mast and place it on the boom. <u>Let go</u> with your <u>back hand</u>.

1.

3. Remaining on the centreline with your back foot behind the daggerboard, slide your front foot back behind the mast base, <u>foot pointing forwards</u>.

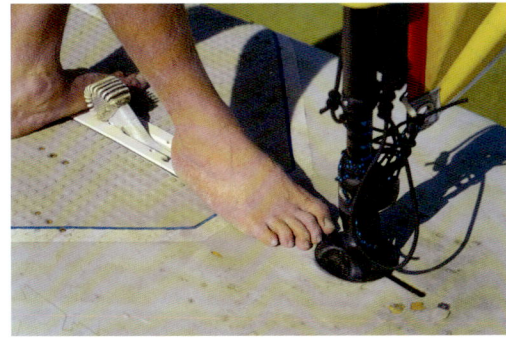

3.

4a. <u>Turn your shoulders towards your goal point</u>, and with an <u>extended (and flexed)</u> front arm, bring the rig to the 'balance point'.

4b. Simultaneously, <u>drop body</u> weight down on a flexed back leg, place the <u>back hand</u> on the boom, and <u>pull in gently</u> to create power.

4a.

5. Continue looking at your goal point, adjust hands and feet, and get comfortable.

6. To stop: release the boom with the back hand and return to the secure position.

5.

Students have learnt a combination of techniques within the 'getting started' section, which has enabled them to sail across the wind, adopt the secure position, turn the board, and now be in the sailing position. It is a golden opportunity to go afloat and consolidate what has been learnt.

Coaching Points

- The balance point is where the rig is placed in a position where the mast is taken beyond vertical, so that it does not require support when released
- Pick a goal point across the wind
- Ensure that the rig is pulled to the balance point, emphasising a smooth, flowing movement throughout
- The power generated by the rig is counterbalanced by body weight
- Power can be *released by easing out with the back hand*, and *increased by pulling in*
- Increase body weight on the back foot as the power increases

On-water One – Sailing Across the Wind

Aim

Instructor demonstrates the 'Getting Started' sequence afloat, allowing the students time afloat to practice and consolidate skills.

Session Structure

1. Sailing across the wind:
    a. Secure position.
    b. Static turn.
    c. Sailing position.
- Allow students time to practise sailing across the wind, allowing mistakes, and providing encouraging refinement and coaching
- When students are competent, continue to Onshore Two

Possible Exercise Suggestions

1. Static turning exercises – either up/downwind or both:
    a) Students to experiment how leaning of the rig turns the board slower or faster.
    b) This can be done in both directions and could be developed into a challenge to see how many static turns they could do in a set amount of time.
2. Sailing position – sailing across the wind using the static turn:
    a) Mark out a small sailing area free of obstructions with some clear goal points for students to aim for.
    b) Keep attempts short so students can stay in the sailing area and also get more input from the Instructor.

Session 5: Onshore One – Steering the Board

Aim

Delivered on a simulator, demonstrating how to steer the board towards and away from the wind, making small adjustments in course, to avoid an object in the water.

Session Considerations

- Provide one demonstration
- Explanations should be kept simple
- Depending on the students' grasp of techniques so far, steering may be introduced within the first water session before being recapped on the simulator

Teaching Sequence

Towards the wind:

1. From the sailing position, look at a goal point slightly closer to the wind.

Away from the wind:

1. From your current sailing position, look back towards your original goal, keeping low.

2. Lean the rig back, extending your back arm.
3. Once you're heading towards your new goal, return to the sailing position, pulling the rig in slightly with your back hand.

2. Keep your back hand pulled in, lean the rig forwards and towards the wind, extending your front arm.
3. The board will turn away from the wind.
4. Once heading back to your original goal, return to the sailing position and ease out using your back hand.

Coaching Points

- The leaning of the rig, forwards or backwards, should be a diagonal action across the board
- Look at your goal point
- Awareness of wind direction

On-water One – Steering

Aim

Instructor demonstration of the 'steering', sequence afloat, allowing the students time afloat to practise and consolidate skills

Possible Exercises

- Sail across the wind and add in steering
- A figure-of-eight course may be useful for students (S-turns)

Teaching Points

- The leaning of the rig, forwards or backwards, should be a diagonal action across the board, enabling a counterbalance of the rig with the body
- Look at your goal point
- Awareness of wind direction

Session 6: Onshore One – Tacking

Aim

Delivered on a simulator, demonstrating how to improve tacking, making the turn more effective and stable, by refining and improving the technique.

Session Considerations

- The students already know the principle of a static turn. These skills can now be refined and improved
- Instructor demonstrates the tack, _once in each direction_

Teaching Sequence

From sailing across the wind:

1.

1.

1. Pick a new goal point further upwind and steer towards it, returning to the sailing position. Remember to pull in with your back hand.
2. Check for obstructions. Place front hand on the mast and front foot in front of the mastfoot.

3.

4.

3. Steer the board towards the wind by leaning the rig back.

4. Once into wind, place both feet in front of the mast and both hands on the mast.
5. Continue turning, just like a static turn.

6. Once back across the wind, return to the sailing position.

6.

Coaching Points

- Checking for obstructions
- Steering to an upwind goal
- When tacking, keep the rig moving across the back of the board

On-water One – Sailing Across the Wind with a 'Tack'

Aim

To develop the tack from a small amount of steering with a static turn to steering slowly further into the wind as the students' wind awareness improves.

Session Exercises

- Follow my leader
- Marked out a course across the wind

Coaching Points

- Checking for obstructions
- Steering to an upwind goal
- Keeping the rig moving across the back of the board

Session 7: Onshore One – Safety

Aim

Delivered ashore and afloat, this session is to raise students' awareness of safety issues and methods of self-rescue. Self-rescue methods are often best demonstrated and practised afloat.

You may choose to introduce safety techniques earlier in order to aid group control and time afloat.

Session Considerations

- Instructor's delivery in providing situations where self-rescue and the alternatives should be considered
- Instructor demonstration of self-rescue ashore or afloat
- Candidates can practise on the water (if appropriate)
- Introduction to seven common senses and:
  - CHECK: the conditions
  - CHECK: your equipment
  - CHECK: yourself

Method 1: Flagging

- A simple and easy route to get back downwind, as well as an effective first introduction to guiding students to sail and steer the board downwind
- Advantages: Possible in any wind strength, quick and easy
- Disadvantages: Not easy to balance in chop, will only take the sailor downwind

Teaching Sequence

1. From the secure position, lean the rig over the nose of the board.
2. Gently lean the sail from side to side to help guide downwind, by steering.
3. By leaning and holding the sail over one side of the nose, the board will steer in the opposite direction.

Method 2: Butterfly Method

- In no wind or light wind, an inability to sail can be easily and quickly remedied with the butterfly method
- Advantages: Very quick and efficient, good for short distances in little or no wind
- Disadvantages: Difficult to maintain the sail balance in choppy conditions, hard to perform on shorter, wider-style beginner boards

Teaching Sequence

1. Make sure the boom is lowered and rest the sail onto the back of the board.
2. Sailor lays on front of board and uses feet to balance sail while paddling.

Session 9: Onshore Two – Upwind Sailing

Aim

Delivered on a simulator, introducing the concept of sailing upwind, demonstrating how this can be achieved by combining sailing closer to the wind with the tacks learnt in Onshore One/On-water One.

Session Considerations

- Instructor provides background theory to upwind sailing:
    - Students given a clear example of the concepts of wind awareness and the 'no-go zone' prior to upwind simulator or on-water demonstration
    - Our sailing line helps us to make progress upwind
- Instructor demonstration:
    - Sailing upwind with clear progression and tacking, _once_ in each direction
    - Introduce and explain the concept and reason for zig-zagging upwind
    - Identify a target directly upwind and explain how progress can be made by holding course on an upwind sailing line with relation to the no-go zone

Teaching Sequence

From the sailing position:

1. Identify and steer towards a goal closer to the wind.
2. Once heading towards your goal, return to the sailing position and pull in with your back hand. _Hold this course_.
3. You are now making progress upwind.
4. Once good progress towards an upwind goal has been achieved, tack and repeat the process until the target is achieved.

Coaching Points

- Awareness of the 'no-go zone'
- Show rig position when sailing upwind
- The importance of zig-zagging upwind to make upwind progression to a realistic target

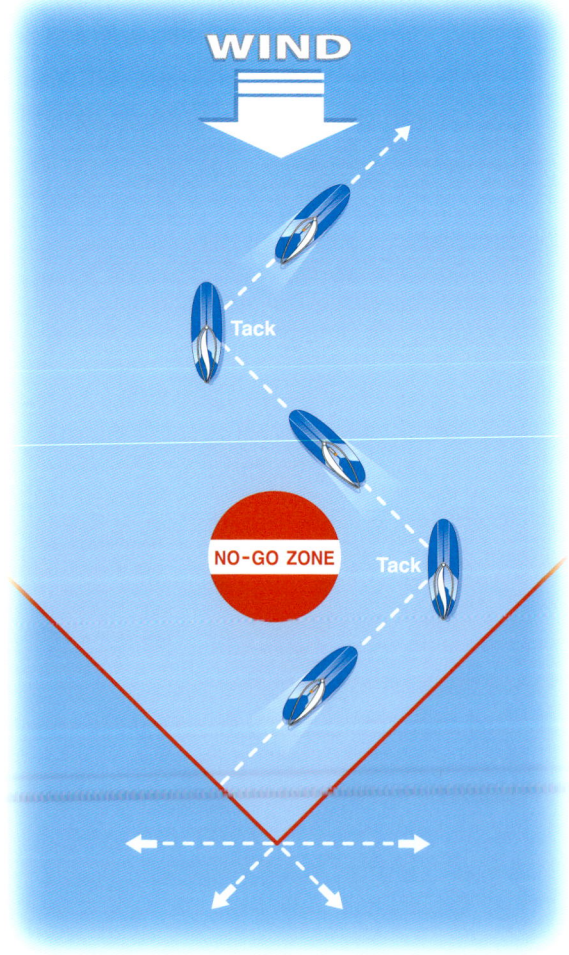

On-water Two – Sailing Upwind

Aim

Introduce the concept of sailing upwind, demonstrating how this can be achieved by combining sailing closer to the wind with the tacks learnt in Onshore One/On-water One, allowing the students time to practise and receive key coaching.

Exercises

The following exercises will assist students in practising the desired techniques. Upwind buoys as goals are useful, provided realistic distances are set:

1. Sailing across the wind (recap if required). Clear markers will help students identify good goal points as they sail across the wind.
2. Upwind and tacking combination. Start with shallow upwind angles, helping students to identify goal points well clear of the 'no-go zone'. These goal points can be made progressively closer to the 'no-go zone' as students develop.

Session 10: Onshore Two – Gybing Downwind

Aim

Delivered on a simulator, demonstrating how to sail downwind and gybe.

Session Considerations

- Instructor should demonstrate <u>twice to reinforce</u>
- <u>*Only* the Instructor demonstrates</u> this section on the simulator
- Students only practise on the water
- Utilise a <u>beginner's simulator with board and rig for Instructor demonstration</u>
- Further coaching should be provided on the water

Teaching Sequence

From a sailing position across the wind:

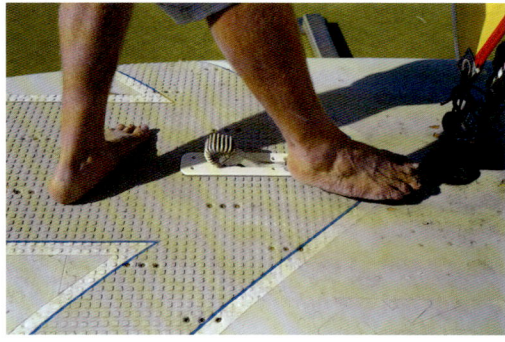

2.

1. <u>Check that the area is clear of obstructions</u>.
2. Step back with the back foot, <u>keep the body low</u>, steer the board away from the wind.
3. Keep leaning the <u>rig across the board until on a run</u>.
4. Once on a run, <u>open the rig</u> by <u>easing out with the back hand</u> so <u>it's square across the board</u>, keeping your head up.

To gybe:

1. <u>Foot change</u>: Move the <u>front foot back</u> in front of the back foot, and move your <u>back foot forwards</u>, <u>keeping weight over the centreline</u>.

1.

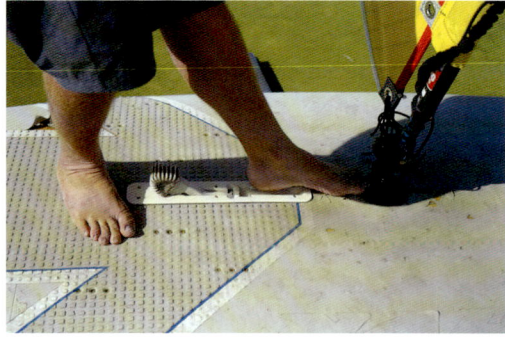

1.

2. <u>Rig change</u>: <u>Slide hand to the boom clamp</u> and release the back hand. Allow the rig to move over the front (nose).
3. As the board <u>turns upwind</u> from a run, and when comfortable to do so, place the new front hand on the other side of the boom, releasing the 'old' front hand.
4. Complete the gybe by leaning the rig backwards so that the board is pointing towards the new goal (across the wind). Resume the sailing position and sail away.

Coaching Points

- Reinforce steering
- Keep weight low
- Stepping back in stronger winds
- Keep weight over centreline on foot change
- Importance of keeping the head up to check area is clear and identify a new goal
- Students must not practise on the simulator with an actual sail. However, if needed, they could practise with a 'ghost' rig.

Session 11: Onshore Two – Sailing on a Run

Aim

Progress the students' ability to steer, while making progress downwind on a run

Session Considerations

- A centre may want Instructors to introduce the students to running and steering downwind. Students may find it easier to run and steer on a run once they have experimented with 'flagging' downwind with no power in the rig
- Instructor demonstrates this section on the simulator
- Students practise on the water

Teaching Sequence

Running and steering on a run, from the sailing position.

Running:

1. Steer the board <u>away from the wind</u>, holding this position until the board is pointing downwind and on a run.
2. <u>Ease the sail out with the back hand</u>. At the same time, move the front foot back, placing both feet either side of the centreline.
3. The sail is now across (at 90 degrees) the centreline of the board. This is <u>running</u>.

Steering:

1. By transferring body weight and/or <u>leaning the rig to the left</u>, the front of the board will turn right.
2. By transferring body weight and/or <u>leaning the rig to the right</u>, the front of the board will turn to the left.

1.

2.

3. If body weight and rig are kept over the <u>centreline of the board</u>, it will continue in a straight line.
4. <u>In stronger winds</u>, <u>move body weight further back</u> on the board and bend the knees to maintain balance and control.
5. To change direction: gybe and resume the sailing position.

Coaching Points

- Reinforce steering
- Keep weight low
- Stepping further back in stronger winds
- While on a run, feet should be either side of the centreline, pointing forward

On-water Two – Sailing Downwind and Gybing

Aim

Provide an on-water demonstration of how to sail downwind and gybe, followed by time afloat for students to practise and receive coaching tips, consolidating all manoeuvres learnt, sailing on all points of sailing, tacking and gybing as needed.

Session Structure

- Instructor to provide on-water demonstration, if required
- Provide individual coaching during a series of upwind and downwind exercises
- Set a good sailing area to help group control and enable your students to use their newly learnt techniques, which mean they make progress:
    - Upwind
    - Downwind
    - Using tacking and gybing as needed
- The limits can be achieved by setting a course or point to aim for, such as a simple journey or course covering all points of sailing, requiring both tacks and gybes

Exercises

1. Steering and power control towards or away from the wind. Practising holding course and making steps towards and away from the wind (zig-zagging downwind and gybing combination).
2. Steering downwind and gybing exercises.
3. Follow my leader. Particularly appropriate for developing and refining upwind work.

Having completed this exercise demonstrating these techniques, students should demonstrate their skill to maintain their position, sail across the wind, make way towards an upwind goal, and return sailing downwind.

Teaching Sequence

Instructor to demonstrate sequences afloat in sections:

1. Sailing upwind.
2. Sailing downwind and gybing.
3. Sailing on a run.

Provide students with time to practise, allow mistakes, and encourage refinement and coaching.

Power Control Downwind

A student is struggling with power in the rig when steering downwind. To achieve a gybe, do progressively deeper steers downwind without actually doing a gybe. This helps students build confidence and the Instructor can increase the amount steered each time until students go through the downwind position and complete a gybe.

THE INTERMEDIATE WINDSURFING TEACHING SYSTEM

The following pages provide Instructors with examples of structured sessions, covering specific techniques utilising the RYA coaching model. These sessions aim to improve on the basic skills students learnt during their Start Windsurfing/Youth Stages 1 and 2 courses, progressing students to Intermediate Windsurfing/Stages 3 and 4. The sessions will also assist Instructors to make the transition from a Start to Intermediate Instructor.

Intermediate is the first level where the coaching model is introduced, aiding a smooth progression from the techniques learnt during the Start Windsurfing course. To ensure a seamless advance, introduce the model as one of the first sessions delivered.

Further information on the RYA coaching model is on pages 101–102.

For many students this is an exciting stage of their windsurfing career, so Instructors must make it a fun and enjoyable experience.

Equipment is Key

One of the key elements is the equipment we use during the course and how we introduce it. Initially, students may find this transition a little daunting, and a few may feel their progression has stepped back rather than improved. However, with specific coaching tips they will quickly be able to overcome this minor hurdle.

The Intermediate Windsurfing course and clinics should be taught on modern equipment, which is essential at this stage of a student's development. Boards should initially be of a volume around 190 to 170 litres, fitted with footstraps and in early stages continue to have a daggerboard, progressing on to a fully battened rig, fitted with harness lines.

Intermediate Simulators

Many new techniques will be introduced on an intermediate or basic stance simulator, a necessity when teaching Intermediate and advanced levels of the syllabus. The design should be sufficient for teaching techniques such as harness work, footstraps, and the RYA coaching model.

- Familiarity to the students is essential. The best option is to utilise modern, durable boards similar to the one students will be using on the water
- Lack of sheltered space often dictates that a rig without a sail is used. However, when possible you should use a small, fully-battened rig
- A pulley system is essential, such as a length of shock cord made into several loops with shackles on each end with a webbing adjustment

- A safety leash which is fitted to three points:
    1. From the main structure.
    2. Halfway along the pulley system.
    3. If possible, on the boom.

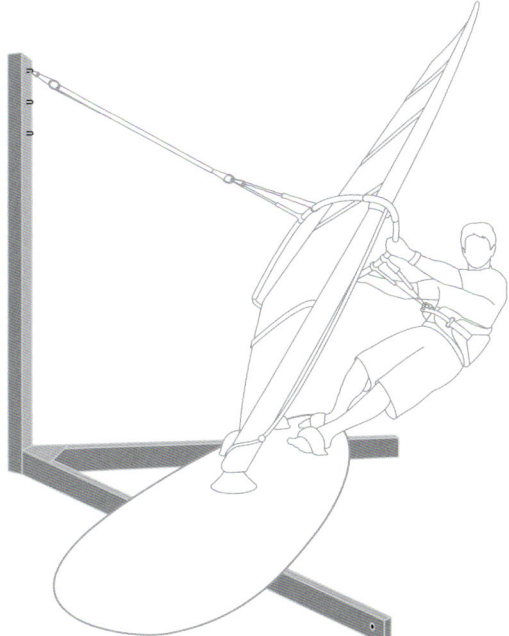

- The board should be placed on a soft surface or welded structure, in a position that allows the student to face the Instructor (looking upwind). It should also be easily changed to enable a beam to a broad reach
- The pulley system can be adjusted for the size of each student and changes in wind strength and direction

Transitions Simulator

A useful simulator and easy to construct – it's just a board with a rig in a clear area. Placing a mat or board bag under the board will enable the simulator to be manoeuvred through all points of sail as the transition is demonstrated or practised.

RYA Intermediate Teaching Sessions

At this stage, there is a wider selection of sessions to choose from dependent on the group's ability and conditions. There is also no set order for the following sessions to be delivered; weather conditions and the individual's/group's ability should play a factor in which techniques are covered when. However, there are a few techniques that you may wish to introduce earlier than others, such as:

- Launching and landing: Brief overview
- Tacking: A good initial session to get people afloat, warm up, and assess ability
- Introduction to the coaching model

Intermediate Sessions

1. Introducing the coaching model.
2. Preparing to launch:
   a. Rigging.
   b. Launching and landing.
3. Tacking.
4. Stance.
5. Getting going.
6. Steering.
7. Harness.
8. Footstraps.
9. Blasting control.
10. Beachstart.
11. Non-planing carve gybe.

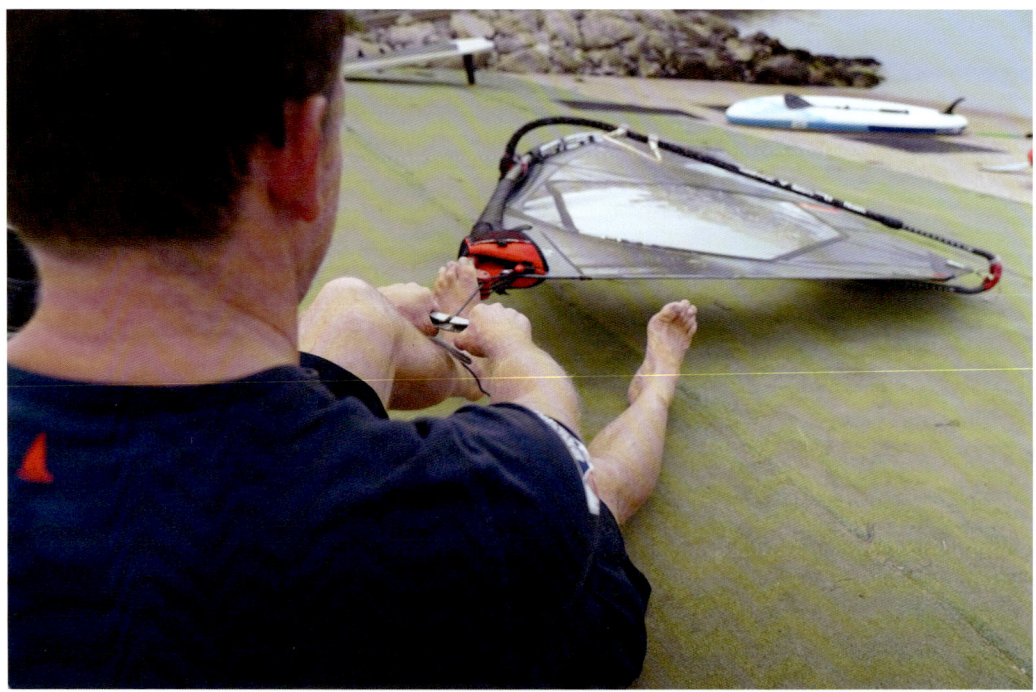

Session One: Introduction to the Coaching Model

Aim

To explain the RYA coaching model terminology by practical demonstration, showing how the elements of the formula fit together and providing a brief outline of the key elements.

A recap will be provided at a later stage, so the initial introduction must be simple and effective, using few words.

Session Considerations

- An Instructor demonstration introducing each element of the coaching formula, based around a simulator
- Describe what it is, *why, when,* and *how* you use it
- Keep the session short – remember you want to get onto the water
- By the end of the session students should have:
  - An understanding of the Fastfwd coaching formula
  - A basic understanding of the key elements
  - An understand of how the formula fits into other areas of their sailing

Teaching Sequence

1. **Vision:** Maintains our sailing line.
   - **What:** How you use your head
   - **Why:** It is the most important part of the formula
     - Where you look is where you go
     - It controls the other parts of the formula
   - **How:**
     - Look upwind for control, decelerate, steer upwind or tack entries
     - Look downwind to accelerate, steer downwind or enter gybes
     - Avoids 'gear gazing' at the harness and footstraps etc.

2. **Trim:** Keeps the board flat.
   - **What:** Board can be kept flat, front to back 'pitch' and side to side 'tilt'
   - **Why:** A flat board is a fast board and a more stable platform
   - **How:** Light winds forwards and inboard
     - Stronger winds move out and back
     - Heel pressure when overpowered or steering upwind
     - Toe pressure when underpowered or steering downwind
     - Once in the straps, flexing the back leg helps to keep the board flat

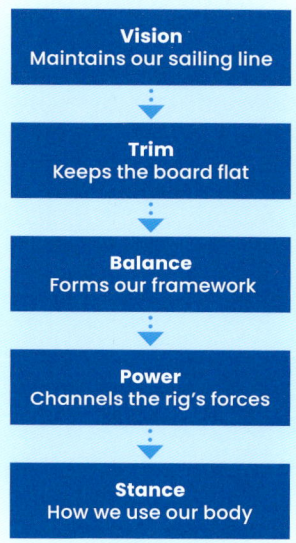

Vision
Maintains our sailing line

Trim
Keeps the board flat

Balance
Forms our framework

Power
Channels the rig's forces

Stance
How we use our body

3. **Balance:** Forms our framework.
   - **What:** The action of using our weight against the movement, power, and weight in the rig
   - **Why:** Keeps the rig away from us, easier to manoeuvre, steer, and generate power
   - **How:** Extended front arm
   - **How:** Counterbalance – move your body and hips in the opposite direction to the rig, for example in transitions

4. **Power:** Channels the rig's forces.
   - **What:** The action of sheeting in, back, and down
   - **Why:** It helps trim the sail and keeps the board flat, as well as being a key part of many windsurfing skills
   - **How:** The front arm must first be extended to help sheet in effectively
   - In stronger winds, sink hips back and down to sheet in
   - In lighter winds, sink hips in and down

5. **Stance:** How we use our body.
   - **Why:** Wind isn't consistent, so we need to adjust our body position through gusts and lulls
   - **How:** By applying the rest of the formula for the wind strength
   - Think about how to position head, hands, hips, and heels

Coaching Points

- To enable the students to start applying and understanding the key elements of the model, start with a move which all students are familiar with, such as a tack
- Encouraging your students to apply the model to their own sailing will ensure the best success. Wherever possible, use real examples to help highlight their importance

Session Two: Rigging

Aim

Reinforce correct setup for the students' boards and rigs, and ensure they are aware of how important it is to have their equipment tuned correctly to suit them and the conditions.

Session Considerations

- A land-based session, preparing the candidates to go afloat
- Consider the level of the students and what is relevant to them at this stage
- Further areas can be recapped at a later stage

By the end of the session, students should have some basic knowledge of board and rig tuning.

Teaching Sequence

- Rigging and tuning:
  - Types of rig
  - Mast
  - Rigging sequence:
    - Apply *some* downhaul
    - Attach boom and apply *some* outhaul
    - Tune downhaul
    - Adjust to correct boom height
    - Check batten tension
    - Tune outhaul tension
  - Basic sail tuning
  - Harness line positioning, width, and length
- Board setup:
  - Intermediate boards (including volume and characteristics)
  - Footstraps placement and adjustment
  - Mast base placement
  - Daggerboard
- Introduction to harness types and fit, and harness lines

Coaching Points

- This session can be extended or shortened to suit weather conditions
- Breaking into smaller setup and tuning sessions before you go afloat will complement further learning, for example footstrap setup before the footstraps session etc.

Session Three: Launching and Landing

Aim

To introduce a safe and secure method of leaving equipment ashore and when taking it afloat, including how to launch and land.

Session Considerations

- Provide an Instructor demonstration
- Practically delivered session
- Include how to manoeuvre equipment on and off the water, securing it ashore safely
- Working in pairs may be a consideration, depending on the strength and ability of the students to carry the board and rig together

Teaching Sequence

Launching:

1. Assessing wind direction and how best to orientate the equipment.
2. How to carry the board and rig together.

Landing:

1. Leaving the water (carrying in reverse).
2. How to carry the board and rig together.

Leaving equipment safety ashore:

1. Wind angle relative to board and sail.
2. Potential hazards of fins pointing up in launching and landing areas.

Coaching Points

- Adaptations should be made depending on the type of kit being used and also the launching area available to the students
- This session also provides an opportunity to get students to start assessing the conditions they will be sailing in, and consider other water users

Session Four: Tacking

Aim

To develop and improve the tack; increasing speed, efficiency, and encourage fewer hand and foot movements.

Session Considerations

- Instructor demonstration (group and location dependent). This might be ashore or afloat, focusing on:
  - Use of a transition simulator: Rig/board without fin to be used on land
  - Importance of vision, counterbalance, and footwork to create the tack. Use a 'Whole-Part-Whole' technique for delivery (see page 40 for more information)
  - Introduction of 'shift and switch'
- Introduction to 'shifting and switching':
  - *Shift* the hip over the front foot that's wrapped around the mast base
  - *Switch* the back foot toe to heel *behind* the front foot
  - Shift the new rear hip and back foot down the board, dropping and pushing

By the end of this session, students should be able to tack faster and more effectively in a range of conditions.

Teaching Sequence

Entry:

1. **Vision:** Look upwind when entering the tack. ....o
2. **Counterbalance:** Front hand on the mast, rig back, body forwards.
3. **Footwork:** Front foot wraps around the mast base.

Midpoint:

1. **Vision:** Head turns to spot old back hand going onto new side of boom, then continues to look at the exit.
2. **Counterbalance:** Mast and body crossover.
3. **Footwork:** 'Shift and switch' the feet.

Exit:

1. **Vision:** Continue to look to the exit of the turn.
2. **Counterbalance:** Rig forwards, body back.
3. **Footwork:** Step back down the board and into a drop and push.

1.

Coaching Points

- Focus on one element at a time: Important areas are vision/counterbalance/footwork.
- Hand on the mast on entry will improve counterbalance
- The lower the front hand goes, the better the pace between body and rig
- While power isn't a key factor, if students slide their back hand in front of the harness lines during the entry it will lead to a slow tack or even going backwards in the middle of the transition

Session Five: Getting Going

Aim

To provide the knowledge and understanding of *how* to accelerate the board, with early steps to getting up on the plane in a range of conditions, under control.

Session Considerations

- Instructor demonstration ashore and afloat
    - Run as a short session (depending on conditions)
    - Reinforce efficient and dynamic body position to encourage early planing in light and strong winds
    - Session afloat, with student practice and Instructor feedback
- Introduce key terms of early planing encouragement: 'drop and dig'/'drop and push'
- Encourage students to experiment with their sailing line, feet, and body positions
- Reinforce the importance of trim, especially on acceleration
- While this session is focussed on the 'drop and push', attention should be given to hand position on the boom and how they are generating balance and power effectively

By the end of this session the student should be able to adopt different body positions in order to get the board going, or even planing earlier.

Teaching Sequence

Get going:

1. **Vision:** Pick the best sailing line to accelerate:
    a. In lighter winds look downwind, stand forwards and inboard, near to the UJ/deckplate.
    b. In stronger winds look across or upwind, standing further back and outboard if the board is still flat.
2. **Trim:** A flat board is a fast board.
3. **Stance:** Introduce term 'drop and push':
    a. The drop: The hips move down and out.
    b. The push: Push through the toes on the front foot.

Once accelerating:

1. **Vision:** Pick new sailing line:
    a. In lighter winds (or if you have control), look across the wind, move feet out slightly and stand up.
    b. In stronger winds, move further out and back on the board as it accelerates.
2. **Trim:** Maintain a flat board by moving feet out and back.

3. **Stance:** Once the board has accelerated, introduce term 'drop and dig':
   a. The drop: The hips move down and out.
   b. The dig: Drive through the heels.
   c. In stronger winds 'drop and dig' to maintain sailing line.

4. Once going, run through the formula to maintain speed and prepare for harness and footstraps.

Coaching Points

- Highlight how getting going or 'dropping and pushing' is used in many different manoeuvres, for example tack exits or steering
- In lighter winds or situations where conditions may be challenging for students, steering or tacking exercises can be used to introduce 'dropping and pushing' as a technique

Session Six: Harness

Aim

To introduce the harness, basic technique, and understanding for setup and line adjustment.

Session Considerations

- Provide an Instructor brief and demonstration covering the following areas:
    - Introduction to the harness, types, and lines
    - Correct rigging, setup, and adjustment
    - Technique for hooking in and out
    - Using hips and stance for board and rig control
    - Safety considerations or briefing, on subjects such as catapults
- Depending on group size and weather conditions it may be appropriate to try the technique on the simulator before going afloat
- This is a good session to encourage the use of larger sails

By the end of this session, students should be able to control 'power' in and out of the harness, enabling them to take the weight off their arms.

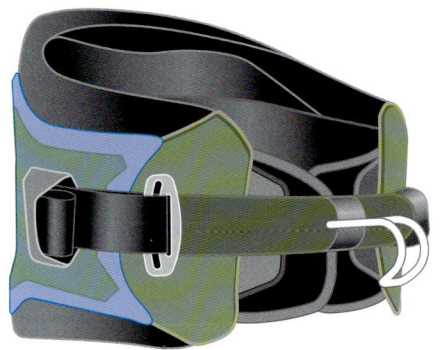 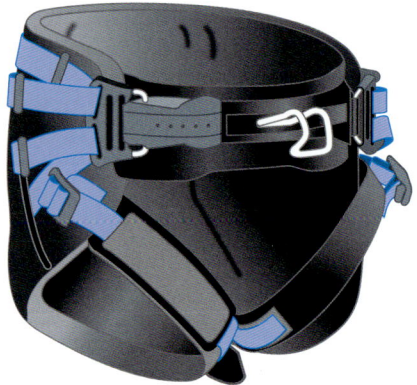

Teaching Sequence

Ashore

Prior to going afloat, provide an Instructor brief, ensuring student involvement:

1. Harness and fitting.
2. Rigging, practical setup of harness lines, and adjustment on student's own equipment.
3. Technique.

Afloat

Hooking in:

1. **Vision:** Look upwind to help bring the harness lines towards you and help control.
2. To hook in, use a short pull on the boom to swing the line towards you while simultaneously lifting hips, then sinking hips into the harness lines.

Once hooked in:

1.

1. **Vision:** Look back towards your sailing line.

2.

2. **Balance:** Extend the front arm to keep the rig away.

3.

3. **Power:** Sink the hips down and out in harness using hips to control the power.

4.

4. **Stance:** Continue to adjust stance for the conditions.

Hooking out:

1. Use a short pull 'in and down' on the boom while simultaneously lifting hips 'up and out'.
2. Re-establish sailing line and stance once unhooked.

Coaching Points

- Heading slightly upwind will make it easier to hook in for the first time
- Experiment with sailing line to control power and bring rig closer to body
- Focus should be on a good stance before hooking in and re-establishing that stance after they have hooked in
- Key focus will be looking back towards where they want to go, and using the hips to control power

Session Seven: Footstraps

Aim

To introduce the technique, progressing towards the use of footstraps.

Session Considerations

- Provide an Instructor brief and simulator demonstration:
  - Cover technique theory: Point of sailing etc.
  - Introduce the footstrap and correct fitting/setup
  - Progressive footwork
- When afloat, ensure there is enough sailing area and conditions to plane:
  - If the wind is too light, a lot of valuable information can still be covered

Teaching Sequence

1. Position and setup of straps:
   a. Inboard vs outboard.
   b. Footstrap size.

1.

2. Front strap:
   a. **Vision:** Looking across or off the wind to help acceleration.
   b. **Trim:** Front foot by front strap.
   c. **Counterbalance:** Focus on counterbalance – rig forwards, body back.

2.

3. Back strap:
   a. **Vision:** Looking upwind to change sailing line.
   b. **Trim:** Back foot by back strap.
   c. **Counterbalance:** Focus on counterbalance – body forwards, rig back.
   d. Focus is on good counterbalance and maintaining sailing line.

3.

4. Safety considerations:
   a. **Sailing line:** For the front strap, the lighter the wind the further away from the wind we aim. Only 5–10 degrees off the wind.
   b. For the back strap, the stronger the wind the further upwind we aim. Only 5–10 degrees towards the wind.

4.

Coaching Points

For sessions in lighter winds, develop techniques through exercises such as:

- Lifting feet up, or leg drags
- Trying to get into the straps in non-planing conditions, all while trying to maintain sailing line

Session Eight: Blasting Control

Aim

Introduce the use of stance as a range, adapting to different conditions while blasting.

Session Considerations

- Provide an Instructor brief and demonstration:
  - Use a simulator reinforced with on-water demos
  - A stance and stance-range recap may be required
  - Introduce spotting gusts and lulls to aid and anticipate stance changes
  - Introduce changes in stance, using terms such as 'drop and dig'
  - These should be run as short sessions covering both light- and strong-wind control
- Provide the students with frequent opportunities reinforced with coaching, feedback, and encouragement

By the end of this session, students should know how to adapt their stance to suit different wind and water conditions by using their full stance range.

Teaching Sequence

Dealing with lulls:

1. **Vision:** Look and head slightly off the wind.
2. Trim: Push through the toes on the front foot to drive the board flat and off the wind.
3. **Balance:** Front arm really extends mast forwards.
4. **Power:** Maintain weight in the harness and keep sheeted in.

Dealing with gusts:

1. **Controlling acceleration:** Super 7 'drop and dig'.
2. **Vision:** Look and head slightly upwind.
3. **Trim:** Dig the heels down.
4. **Stance:** 'Drop and dig'.

Coaching Points

- To allow the students to blast properly when conditions are less favourable, it is probably more beneficial to spend more time on the simulator with students having a go and asking questions
- Alternatively, when developing stance range, use extreme steering exercises to get students to move into a more dynamic body position and start to use their head, hips, and heels to counter the rig

Session Nine: Steering

Aim

Developing the steering technique to be more dynamic, enabling a course to be held using head, body, and rig position.

Session Consideration

- Provide an Instructor demonstration ashore, reinforced with on-water demonstrations
- Background theory
- When students practise afloat, provide continual feedback
- Steering should be introduced as a valuable technique for:
    - Changing direction to alter course or avoid an obstacle
    - Basic technique required for steering in and out of a tack and gybe
    - Sailing a board without a daggerboard upwind
- This session should cover steering, both in and out of the harness and footstraps, making it a session which works regardless of conditions

By the end of this session students should be able to change the board's direction effectively, using their vision, trim, counterbalance, and stance.

Teaching Sequence

Steering: Non-Planing

Upwind: To avoid obstacles and make progress upwind:

1. Vision: Look upwind.
2. Trim: Weight heels on windward rail.
3. Balance: Lean the rig back as body weight moves forwards.
4. Power and stance: Pull in and down on the boom to maintain power and help trim.

Downwind:

1. Vision: Look downwind.
2. Trim: Extend front leg and push hard through toes of front foot.
3. Balance: Extend front arm and angle the mast forwards, move back hand back, sheeting in.
4. Power and stance: 'drop and push'.

Steering: Planing

Upwind:

1. Vision: Look upwind.
2. Trim: Pull up on toes and weight both heels.
3. Counterbalance: Slightly rake the rig back.
4. Counterbalance: Come forwards to counterbalance rig as the board turns into wind.

Downwind:

1. Vision: Look downwind.
2. Trim: Push hard through toes of front foot.
3. Balance: Extend front arm and keep mast forwards.
4. Stance: Sheet the boom in and keep weight down in harness.

Coaching Points

- Reinforce this session as the forerunner to all transitions
- Steering as an exercise is a way to experiment with stance and increase how dynamic a student's body position is
- If moving on to boards without a daggerboard, use these techniques to improve and enhance students' upwind sailing and control

Session Ten: Beachstarts

Aim

Introduce the basic techniques of a beachstart including rig recovering, manoeuvring, power control, and getting onto the board.

Session Considerations

Ashore

- Instructor to provide onshore brief:
  - Include hazards, especially submerged
  - Introduce 'nose over toes' and 'slide and glide'
- Location considerations:
  - If possible, a gently shelving waterbed which drops off gradually
  - Make sure there is sufficient water depth for the boards and fins being used. Use smaller fins where waters are shallow
  - Ensure the launching area is large enough with space between students, especially in stronger winds

Afloat

- Instructor demo ashore introducing the beachstart, followed by student practice and feedback:
  - Beachstart demonstration (afloat)
  - Rig control and manoeuvre demo
- This session can be broken down into manoeuvring the board and rig in the shallows and the actual beachstart itself
- In areas where the launching area is restricted, leg drags can help develop the technique for beachstarts

Teaching Sequence

Instructor demonstration to show all stages of the technique:

1. Handling the rig.
2. Positioning the board/rig.
3. Full beachstart.

Rig manoeuvring:

1. Rig recovery 'sliding and gliding':
   a. Recover the rig from the water by positioning the mast across the wind.
   b. Grab the mast above the boom.
   c. Slide the mast, guiding it across and overhead to windward before lifting.

2. Manoeuvring board and rig in the shallows.

The beachstart (full manoeuvre):

Preparation:

1. Stand near tail of board, looking towards the UJ.
2. In light winds, position the board across the wind.
3. In stronger winds, position the board slightly upwind. Keep the rig low until initiating the rig twist.

1.

Manoeuvre:

1. **Trim:** Position back heel on the board midway between front and back straps.

1.

2. **Balance/power:** The 'rig twisting' action initiates the pull in the rig:
   a. Generate lift by forcing the front hand up and forwards, as the back hand sheets the boom in above the head.

   b. This twisting action creates power which needs to be accentuated, especially in lighter winds.

2b.

c. When our head is moving right in towards the mast base and the rig is more upright, we pull down on the boom.

2c.

3. Vision: 'Nose over toes' as you roll forwards, flex the back leg to come up the board.
4. **Stance:** Once up on the board, stay low.
5. **Stance:** Drop and push underneath the boom to help acceleration.

6. Find your new sailing line and sail away.

6.

Coaching Points

This session can be linked with other techniques that require the student to return repeatedly to the shore and relaunch. Your students are therefore continually practising beachstarts while improving other techniques too.

Session Eleven: The Non-planing Carve Gybe

Aim

To introduce a gybe which can be used in both non-planing and planing conditions, forming the platform and progression for learning the planing carve gybe.

Session Considerations

- Instructor demonstration ashore and/or afloat:
  - Manoeuvre theory
  - Dry-land simulation of gybing, followed by on-water exercises and Instructor feedback (utilising rig/board without fin to be used on land)
- Afloat:
  - Start the session with a demonstration
  - Break the gybe into sections using the 'Whole-Part-Whole' technique for delivery (see page 40 for delivery)
    - Entry, midpoint, and exit, or hand and footwork
    - Use vision, counterbalance, stance, and footwork
    - Reinforce the 'shift and switch' and 'rig rotator'

By the end of this session, students should be able to turn the board by gybing and breaking down the technique.

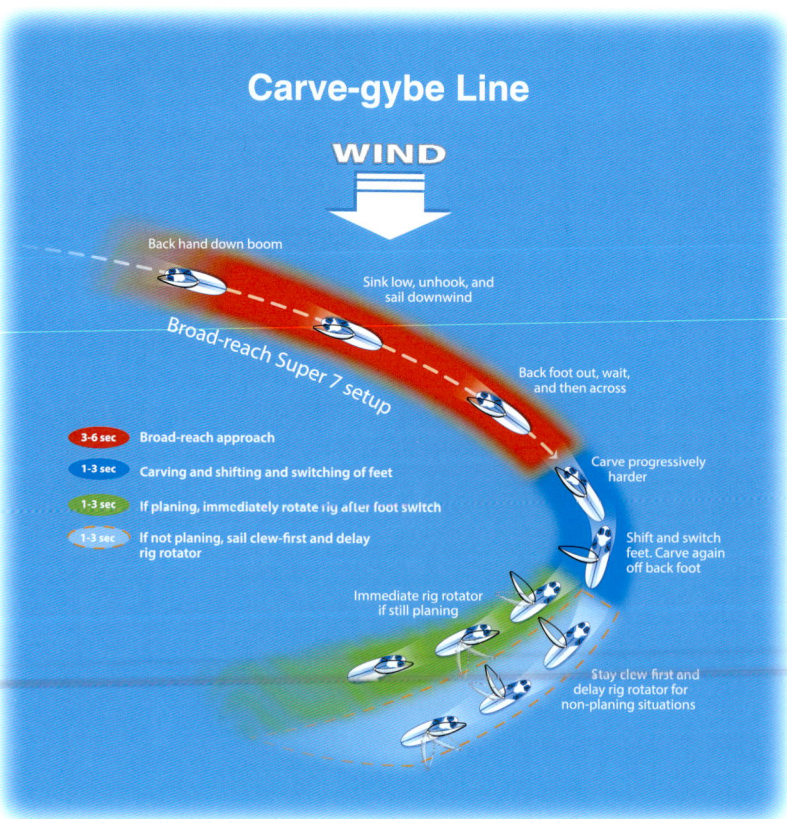

Teaching Sequence

Entry:

1. **Vision:** Look downwind.
2. **Counterbalance:** Rig forwards, body back, back hand down the boom.
3. **Footwork:** Step back and across, 'drop and push'.

Midpoint:

1. **Vision:** Look through and out of the turn.
2. **Counterbalance:** Lean the mast out of the turn (like the rig is splitting the board in half).
3. **Footwork:** Shift and switch the feet as the board reaches or just passes the downwind stage of the gybe.

3.

Exit:

1. **Vision:** Look out of the turn.

2.

2. **Counterbalance:** Slide front hand to boom clamp.

5.

3.

3. **Counterbalance:** Flip the 'rig back, body forwards', 'rig forwards, body back'.
4. **Footwork:** 'Drop and push'.
5. Find your new sailing line and sail away.

Coaching Points

The rig flip may well be a new technique, so time can be spent practising this on land or in light winds using exercises like sail 360s to build confidence.

THE ADVANCED WINDSURFING TEACHING SYSTEM

When providing advanced coaching it's important to refer continually to, use, and improve on the basics developed at the Intermediate stage, reinforcing how the techniques learnt are progressive.

For example, when coaching at advanced level, students who are confident planing in the harness using footstraps on a larger-volume board in marginal winds will develop by coaching them to deal with more challenging conditions (like stronger wind) and lower-volume boards.

Essentially, Instructors develop the students' existing techniques and help them to become more efficient and effective.

Most techniques are a seamless continuation from the Intermediate clinics:

- Beachstarts progress to water starts
- Through encouragement and use of the pre-learned techniques and specific coaching concepts, we can ensure our students experience swift and easy progression.

Advanced Instructors should isolate and perfect the defining techniques that make the difference on the water. Progression to higher levels is often down to developing and refocusing the techniques that students already have.

It is easy to imagine there must be something complicated that needs to be learnt to become a better windsurfer. However, in reality, the best windsurfers are just really good at the basics; it's all about emphasising and honing these.

Below are three major considerations for Advanced Instructors and coaches to think about:

1. Simplify your delivery: Always summarise your coaching suggestions, and break moves or objectives into the key parts (bite-size chunks).
2. On the water, focus on one technique or objective at a time.
3. Always try to sail on your students' equipment to ensure things such as harness-line setup are correct. Fatigue and board-handling problems are vastly exaggerated in stronger winds when gear is set up incorrectly.

Finally, and most importantly, advanced coaching is emphasising even greater commitment to the basics. At higher speeds in more challenging conditions, the amount of processing power available to students is limited, so being skilful at the basic technique consistently makes all the difference.

RYA Advanced Teaching Sessions

Information and sessions to be covered:

- Advanced tack
- Blasting control:
  - Spin out
  - Heading upwind
  - Strong wind/small board uphaul
- Transitioning to smaller boards (including high-wind uphauling)
- Waterstart
- Planing carve gybe
- Advanced carving moves:
  - Duck gybe
  - Laydown gybe
  - Strap-to-strap gybe
- Bump and jump

Session One: Carving Tack

Aim

To improve tacking technique for smaller boards, encouraging the use of foot steering into the tack entry while on the plane.

Session Considerations

Ashore:

- Provide an Instructor land-based simulator session:
    - Fixed simulator: Finless board and rig
- Use land-based exercises:
    - Foot movement
    - Rig movement

Afloat:

- Instructor demonstration
- Light- or high-wind exercises afloat:
    - Progressively carving into wind in planing conditions
    - Steering exercises and back-winded tacks in lighter winds
- Individual feedback:
    - 'Whole-Part-Whole' delivery is fundamental in helping students achieve this technique
    - While we are progressing the tack from Intermediate, the sequence of the preparation is different and will need breaking down further

Teaching Sequence

Preparation:

1. Look upwind, and check the area is clear to tack.
2. Still hooked in, move front hand onto mast.
3. Unhook, sink low, rig back, body forwards.
4. Carve upwind, keep the board flat front to back by moving feet forwards:
    a. Note: Taking the back foot out of the strap will be dependent on wind strength.
    b. In stronger winds the back foot stays in longer.
    c. The front foot stays in the front strap until ready to transition.

Entry:

1. **Vision:** Look upwind.
2. **Counterbalance:** Maintain rig back, body forwards.
3. **Foot work:** Back foot moves forwards as the board carves into wind. The front foot wraps round the mastfoot just before the midpoint.

Entry

Midpoint:

1. **Vision:** Spot the hand moving across and look straight to the exit.
2. **Counterbalance:** Back hand moves straight to the new side, maintain space.
3. **Foot work:** Shift and switch weight around the mastfoot.

Exit:

1. **Vision:** Look out of the turn.
2. **Counterbalance:** Let the front hand slide back, rig forwards, body back.
3. **Footwork/stance:** Step back down the board, drop weight, and push through toes on the front foot.

Midpoint

Exit

Coaching Points

- Focus on one element at a time, important areas are: vision, counterbalance, and footwork
- The board will stop carving into wind as soon as the front foot wraps around the mastfoot. Students should experiment with carving further and further into wind:
  - Try progressively carving into wind, delaying the timing of the foot movement
- The lower the front hand is on the mast on entry, the better the counterbalance
- Focus on students trying to move across the board

Session Two: Blasting Control (Including Improved Stance)

Aim

Improve the stance on smaller boards, adapting to different conditions and points of sail to enhance blasting control.

Session Considerations

Provide an Instructor brief and demonstration:

- Provide sailing-theory knowledge on apparent wind and centre of effort vs centre of lateral resistance
- Use a simulator reinforced with on-water demos:
    - Recap on stance and stance ranges
    - Discuss the impact of fin size and setup on blasting control.
    - Reinforce and develop dynamic stance actions 'drop and push' and 'drop and dig'
- This technique should be run as short sessions covering both light- and strong-wind control
- Provide the students with frequent opportunities reinforced with coaching, feedback, and encouragement

By the end of this session students should know how best to adapt their stance to suit different wind and water conditions by using their full stance range, on all points of sail.

Teaching Sequence

Getting going on smaller boards:

1. **Vision:** Look forwards and head five–10 degrees downwind.
2. **Trim:** Keep feet forwards, inboard, and push through forwards-facing toes of the front foot. This may mean both feet are in front of the front straps!
3. **Balance:** Make sure the front hand is by the harness lines and fully extend the front arm to assist trim.

4. **Power:** Back hand back, sheet in, back and down on the boom.

Combining these points correctly will create the elements of a Super 7 'drop and push' body position, heavily flexing the rear leg. As the board accelerates, quickly shift out and back into the straps.

Blasting upwind:

1. **Vision:** Look upwind.
2. **Trim:** Roll weight forwards, onto the outside of the front foot, digging through the front heel.
3. **Counterbalance:** Rig back as body weight goes forwards.
4. **Power:** Stay sheeted in with weight against the front of the harness.
5. **Stance:** Maintain hips out with an upright body, using hips and legs to deal with gusts and lulls.

Dealing with 'lulls':

1. **Vision:** Look and head slightly off the wind.
2. **Trim:** Push through the toes on the front foot to drive the board flat and off the wind.
3. **Balance:** Front arm really extends mast forwards.
4. **Power:** Maintain weight in the harness and keep sheeted in.

Dealing with 'gusts':

1. **Controlling acceleration:** Super 7 'drop and dig'.
2. **Vision:** Look and head slightly upwind.
3. **Trim:** Dig the heels down.
4. **Stance:** 'Drop and dig'.

'Spin out' generally occurs due to a number of reasons revolving around equipment setup, trim, balance, and power (plus stance). So Instructors *must* ensure:

- Equipment:
  - The downhaul is set correctly and the rig is set correctly
  - The fin for the sail size or power is correct
  - Harness lines are set far enough back
- Trim:
  - They flex the back leg or both legs to keep the board flat on the water
  - Students drive the rear foot against the fin appropriately
- Balance and power:
  - Sail are set correctly and body position is far enough away from the rig
- Stance:
  - The back leg is bent and weighted correctly, especially at speed. Must flex the back leg in anticipation of chop
  - Must be in the correct position
  - Look for Super 7 'drop and dig' in stronger winds

Coaching Points

- Check student's position of head, hands, hips, and heels to provide specific individual feedback
- Encourage students to bring hands together and focus weight in the harness by pushing hips out to engage their legs more
- At advanced level, students should use their legs as the primary way of adjusting stance across different wind strengths and water states

Session Three: High-wind Uphauling

Aim

To enable transitioning to smaller boards, dramatically reduce the fatigue of uphauling in planing winds or on lower-volume boards.

Session Considerations

- Practical demonstration afloat
- This exercise can be run as a light-wind session linked with safety, or as a demo when taking non-waterstarting students out in planing winds
- This session is particularly useful for:
  - Uphauling in planing winds or on choppy waters
  - Uphauling on lower-volume boards if the wind has suddenly dropped
  - Developing existing uphauling technique with the emphasis on heading and staying upwind during and after uphauling

Teaching Sequence

1. **Vision:** Look <u>upwind</u> to keep and turn the board upwind when uphauling.
2. **Trim:** Front foot just in front of mastfoot, back foot near or between front straps.
3. **Trim:** On wider boards or with bigger rigs, engage the rail to help release the rig.
4. <u>Pushing through the feet</u> to point the board above a beam reach, rig back, body forwards to initially head upwind and smoothly release the rig from the water.
5. As the rig clears, <u>the rig is kept into wind</u> to help it lift.
6. <u>Forward movement</u> of the rig makes it more stable when grabbing the boom.
7. **Stance:** <u>Stay low</u> and use the legs to uphaul, looking forwards and low as soon as the boom is in the hands.

Coaching Points

- Foot positioning may vary on different boards, with feet needing to be more outboard on wider-style boards or those with bigger rigs
- Lengthening the uphaul rope can initially make the uphaul process easier and more stable
- Focus on letting the board turn into wind. This technique reduces wobble and students will find it easier to balance and sheet in on a lower-volume board, rough water, and/or stronger winds

Session Four: Waterstart

Aim

Transition from beachstarts to the waterstart in deeper water, enabling the sailor to progress to lower volume boards and a wider variety of conditions.

Session Considerations

- This session can be run as part of an advanced course or as a specific session or clinic, either in a one-to-one or group session
- The beachstarting techniques are transferred and progressed to aid learning the waterstart
- An Instructor should demonstrate the technique by breaking it down into four specific areas:
    1. <u>Board and rig orientation</u>: Rules of board and rig orientation in deeper water
    2. <u>Rig elevation</u>: 'Sliding and guiding' the rig to clear it from the water
    3. <u>Generating lift</u>: 'Rig twisting' and orientation using balance and power
    4. <u>Specific vision</u>: 'Nose over toes' to minimise body weight on the rig

By the end of this session, the students should be able to:

- Fly the rig without standing on the ground
- Correctly position the board and rig
- Create lift from the rig to help bring themselves in towards and up onto the board
- Understand the correct body position to maximise the rig's lift

Teaching Sequence

Board and rig orientation:

1. <u>Keep back to the wind</u> with the equipment downwind.
2. When recovering the rig, always <u>handle the mast</u>.
3. <u>The more submerged the rig, the further up the mast we start</u>.
4. Swim the mast towards the wind.

Rig elevation by 'sliding and guiding' the rig:

1. Always elevate the rig with the mast at <u>90 degrees to the wind</u>.
2. Hold the mast approximately one metre above the boom clamp and get a good distance from the mast by extending the front arm.
3. To release the rig clear of the water, wiggle or shake the mast to break the surface tension.
4. In <u>one</u> strong movement, kick positively with the feet to keep the head above the water, <u>simultaneously</u> 'sliding and guiding' the mast across over the head as far to windward as possible, and only then up. Refrain from lifting the mast straight up as this can cause the body to go down, or the clew to catch.
5. The mast should move from a stretched-out arm position downwind to a stretched-out position upwind of you.
6. Once the rig is guided to windward and has cleared the water, the back hand grabs the boom.

6.

Generating lift by 'rig twisting':

1. To create lift, the front hand pushes up and forwards as the back hand sheets the boom in above the head, creating a 'twisting action' with the whole rig.

The waterstart (the whole manoeuvre):

1. In controllable conditions, position the upper body upwind of the tail with the board across the wind.
2. In stronger winds, position the board slightly upwind.

3.

4.

3. Trim: With the rig high, place the rear heel just to windward of the centreline between the straps.

4. **Balance/power:** Use the 'rig twister' to generate lift.
5. **Vision:** Use nose over toes to keep weight going forwards.
6. **Trim:** Bring the front foot on once you are approaching fully upright.

7. **Stance:** Stay low once on the board, drop, and push.

7.

Coaching Points

Common problems/solutions:

- Lifting the mast straight up and catching the clew:
  - Guide the mast more to windward while recovering the rig
- Board spinning into wind by over-extending or weighting the back leg when bringing the back foot up onto the board:
  - Focus on just the heel starting on the board
- Focus heavily on nose over toes to stop the head coming up above the boom
- Only being lifted partially out:
  - Often caused by bringing the front foot up too soon. Try delaying this for as long as possible, even doing leg-drag exercises to reinforce

Session Five: Planing Carve Gybe

Aim

Developing the 'non-planing carve gybe' into the 'planing carve gybe'.

Session Considerations

Preparation is the key consideration with the transition progressing and following a similar sequence, but at higher speeds. Many of the areas requiring exaggeration in the non-planing version do not require as much in the planing version.

- Instructor land-based demonstration:
    - Utilise a stance or static simulator, finless board, and rig
    - Footwork development with 'shift and switch'
- Run land-based exercises:
    - Carving the board without the rig
    - Footwork exercises
    - Rig-flip exercises
- Light- or high-wind exercises afloat:
    - Non-planing carve gybe
    - Sail 360s
    - Bearing away and holding speed unhooked
    - Gybing with increasing speed
- 'Whole-Part-Whole' delivery will be fundamental in helping students achieve this technique. Developing this technique may take several sessions over a period of time
- By the end of this session students should be able to:
    - Set up, unhook, and control entry to the gybe
    - Apply pressure to carve the board
    - Time foot change and rig flip
    - Turn the board through a planing carve gybe

Teaching Sequence

Preparation:

1. Check the area is clear, especially downwind.
2. Keep the front hand back.
3. Back hand down the boom, sheet in, and sink low in the harness (if in the harness, unhook).
4. 'Drop and push' to bear the board away.
5. Back foot out and across the board.

Entry:

1. **Vision:** Look into the turn.
2. **Counterbalance:** Rig forwards and across, back hand sheeted in.
3. **Foot work/stance:** Roll across the board, sink weight to the inside of the turn with soft knees, front foot still in the strap.

Midpoint:

1. **Vision:** Keep looking to the inside of the turn.
2. **Counterbalance:** Open the rig to the outside of the turn, keeping body to the inside.
3. **Footwork/stance:** Shift and switch your feet to stay carving.

Exit:

1. **Vision:** Look to the exit.
2. **Counterbalance:** Let the front hand slide to the boom clamp, rig back, body forwards on the rig flip, collect the rig with the new front hand going underneath.
3. **Stance:** Once you collect the rig, drop and push, keep the board carving.

Coaching Points

- Light-wind drills will improve the chances of success. Concentrate on:
  - Rig flip
  - Footwork, 'shift and switch'
- Adjusting equipment can further aid progression:
  - Larger boards with smaller rigs will turn through a wider arc, making the move slower and easier to process
- Rig flip: By placing the _new_ front hand underneath the position of the _old_ front hand, it will aid in keeping body weight low
- The planing carve gybe: Ensure sailing angle and timing are correct, as they both play as much of a fundamental part as technique

Planing Gybe: 'Shift and Switch'

Entry: Back foot across, just in front of back strap.

Midpoint: Just after downwind feet come heel to toe, quickly step forwards, keeping the board carving.

Exit: Stepping forwards to flatten the board, dropping and pushing to hold power.

Session Six: Advanced Carving – Duck Gybe

Aim

Introducing a variety of carving moves beyond the 'planing carve gybe'.

Session Considerations

- Instructor brief and land-based demonstration:
    - Preparation is similar in all carving moves
    - Utilise a stance or static simulator, finless board, and rig
- Run land-based exercises:
    - Ducking the rig
    - Sailing switch
    - Foot-change exercises
- Light- or high-wind exercises afloat:
    - Non-planing duck gybe
    - Sail 360s
    - Clew-first sailing
    - Strap-to-strap gybes
    - Duck gybing
- 'Whole-Part-Whole' delivery will be fundamental in helping students achieve this technique
- Developing this technique may take several sessions over a period of time

By the end of this session, students should be able to:

- Setup, unhook, and control entry to the duck gybe
- Time the duck
- Maintain the board carving through the turn
- Exit switch and change the feet

Teaching Sequence

Preparation:

1. Check the area is clear (especially downwind).
2. Keep the front hand back, by the harness lines.
3. Back hand down the boom, sheet in, and sink low in the harness (if in the harness, unhook).
4. *'Drop and push'* to bear the board away.
5. Back foot out and across the board.

Entry:

1. **Vision:** Look into the turn.
2. **Counterbalance:** Duck the rig:
   a. Extend and release the front hand, pushing the mast forwards and to the inside of the turn.
   b. Cross the original front hand over with the back hand, on the same side of the boom.
   c. Throw the clew to the outside of the turn.
   d. Grab the new side of the boom as far up as possible and keep the rig opened up.

3. **Footwork/stance:** Roll across the board, sink weight to the inside of the turn with soft knees, front foot still in the strap.

Midpoint:

1. **Vision:** Keep looking to the inside of the turn.
2. **Counterbalance:** Keep the rig open and continue to carve the board.
3. **Footwork/stance:** Maintain foot position with weight sunk to the inside of the turn.

Exit:

1. **Vision:** Keep looking to the exit.
2. **Counterbalance/power:** Begin to pull in power on a new broad reach, keeping the body weight to the inside of the turn.
3. **Footwork:** Once stable on a new broad reach, 'shift and switch' the feet. Then 'drop and push'.

Coaching Points

- Timing of the duck is the most important consideration in this manoeuvre:
  - Too early and the rig will get thrown into the water
  - Too late and the rig will fail to duck successfully
- Work on preparation and entry to achieve timing success

Session Seven: Advanced Carving – Laydown Gybe

Aim

Introducing a progression from the standard carve gybe, utilised for performance sails and stronger winds

Session Considerations

- Instructor brief and land-based demonstration:
  - Preparation is very similar in all carving moves
  - Utilise a stance or static simulator, finless board, and rig
- Run land-based exercises:
  - Laying down the rig
  - Opening and flipping the rig
  - Foot-change exercises with the focus on speed
- Light- or high-wind exercises afloat:
  - Cowboys
  - Sail 360s
  - Heli tacks
  - One-handed laydown gybes
  - Laydown gybes
- 'Whole-Part-Whole' delivery will be fundamental in helping students achieve this technique. Developing this technique may take several sessions over a period of time

By the end of this session, students should be able to:

- Set up, unhook, and control entry to the laydown gybe
- Lay the rig down
- Open the rig while changing the feet
- Flip the rig, maintaining speed on

Teaching Sequence

Preparation:

1. Check the area is clear, especially downwind.
2. Keep the <u>front hand back</u>, <u>by the harness lines</u>.
3. Back hand down the boom, sheet in, and sink low in the harness (if in the harness, unhook).
4. 'Drop and push' to bear the board away.
5. Back foot out and across the board.

Entry:

1. **Vision:** Look into the turn.
2. **Counterbalance:** Lay down the sail:
   a. Push down with the front hand while pulling up and *over sheeting* the back hand.

    b. Push head and shoulders forwards to counterbalance while still carving the board.

    c. Once the rig is laid down, start to bring it back up by opposing its weight with your body.

3. **Footwork/stance:** Roll across the board, sink weight to the inside of the turn with soft knees, front foot still in the strap.

Midpoint:

1. **Vision:** Keep looking to the inside of the turn.
2. **Counterbalance:** Open the rig and throw the body to the inside of the turn.
3. **Footwork/stance:** Shift and switch the feet.

Exit:

1. **Vision:** Look to the exit.
2. **Counterbalance:** Let the front hand slide to the boom clamp, rig back, body forwards on the rig flip, collect the rig with the new front hand going underneath.
3. **Stance:** Once you collect the rig, drop and push, keep the board carving.

Coaching Points

- Speed of the laydown is the most important consideration
- Getting the mast to drop to the inside of the turn is controlled by front-hand position and extension
- The laydown tightens the turn, so the speed of the rig opening, foot change, and flip will need to increase
- Additional sessions like Clew First Waterstart may be useful

Session Eight: Advanced Carving – Downwind 360

Aim

Fun manoeuvre enhancing board and sail control

Session Considerations

- Instructor brief and land-based demonstration:
    - Preparation is very similar in all carving moves
    - Utilise a stance or static simulator, finless board, and rig
- Run land-based exercises:
    - Laying down the rig
    - Stepping up from being back-winded
    - Midpoint rig position
- Light- or high-wind exercises afloat:
    - Back-winded sailing
    - Back-winded tacks
    - One-handed laydown gybes
    - One-handed downwind 360s
    - Downwind 360s
- 'Whole-Part-Whole' delivery will be fundamental in helping students achieve this technique. Developing this technique may take several sessions over a period of time

By the end of this session, students should be able to:

- Set up, unhook, and control entry to the downwind 360
- Lay the rig down
- Carve the board past downwind
- Step up from back-winded and control the end of the turn.

Teaching Sequence

Preparation:

1. Check the area is clear, especially downwind.
2. Keep the <u>front hand back, by the harness lines</u>.
3. Back hand down the boom, sheet in, and sink low in the harness (if in the harness, unhook).
4. 'Drop and push' to bear the board away.
5. Back foot out and across the board.

Entry:

1. **Vision:** Look forwards.
2. **Counterbalance:** Lay down the sail.
3. **Footwork/stance:** Roll across the board, sink weight to the inside of the turn with soft knees, front foot still in the strap.

Midpoint:

1. **Vision:** Look at the mast tip.
2. **Counterbalance:** Maintain the rig laid down and pull it back over the tail of the board, weight moving forwards.
3. **Footwork/stance:** Continue carving.

Exit:

1. **Vision:** Keep the head up.
2. **Counterbalance:** Keep the rig back, push out, back, and down turning into wind. Bear away once wind is on the new side of the sail.
3. **Footwork:** Step up with the front foot and control out of the turn.

Coaching Points

- Angle and timing of sweeping the rig back are key considerations
- The rig needs to be swept *well* back to help turn the board. It should be making contact with the rear shin

Session Nine: Bump and Jump

Aim

To enhance control and confidence in choppy conditions, and learning to jump the board clear of the water and land in control.

Session Considerations

- Instructor brief and land-based demonstration:
    - Use a finless board and rig
    - Sailing angle is a key consideration
- Run land-based exercises:
    - The jumping foot movement
    - Feeling wind under the windward edge of the board
- Checking through equipment setup:
    - Fin size
    - Footstrap size
- Light- or high-wind exercises afloat:
    - Extreme steering/flat-water wave riding
    - Changing board trim with feet
    - Chop hopping
- 'Whole-Part-Whole' delivery will be fundamental in helping students achieve this technique. Developing this technique may take several sessions over a period of time

By the end of this session, students should be able to:

- Set up kit
- Spot a ramp and unhook in preparation
- Get the board airborne
- Land under control

Teaching Sequence

Takeoff:

1. **Vision:** Look upwind to spot a small wave ahead of you. Head slightly upwind.
2. **Trim:** Move inboard and pull down on the boom.
3. **Balance and power:** Unhook and sink low, with an upright body. Compress ahead of the ramp.
4. **Stance:** Push down with the back foot and extend the front leg up, lifting the windward rail.

In the air:

1. **Vision:** Keep looking ahead.
2. **Trim:** Tuck up with your back leg and extend the front leg, scissoring the board off the wind.
3. **Stance:** Stay tucked up, pulling in and down on the front arm.

Landing:

1. **Stance:** Stay tucked then extend a soft back leg to land.
2. Sheet out slightly as you land.

Coaching Points

- Most success will be had by jumping slightly into wind
- Focus should be getting the nose and windward rail up
- Catapults and failure to jump usually come from taking off too far downwind

THE WINDFoil TEACHING SCHEME

RYA First Flights

Aim

This is the first course in the RYA WINDFoil Scheme, which provides a basic introduction and how to make the first foiling takeoff and glide.

Recommended course duration: Four hours at maximum ratio.

Students: Four.

Foils: Two.

Instructor: One.

Powerboat: One.

Session Considerations

- Personal safety equipment
- Foiling equipment
- Briefing shallow areas
- Approaching, launching, and recovering foil to avoid injury

Sailing Area

When setting up the sailing area, ensure it is deep enough and free from obstacles. Here are a few considerations:

- Ideally they should be upwind of other craft as once students get the hang of foiling they will find sailing upwind the easiest direction of travel
- Boards can easily be sailed non-planing/non-foiling. To get to the area, students can walk out to a set point (of a good minimum depth), most likely uphaul to avoid injury and also due to wind strength, and then get the go-ahead once in the foiling area

Session Dynamics

- The Instructor briefs all students on land
- Two students go out in a RIB with the Instructor
- The remaining students sail out non-planing/non-foiling to the anchored RIB

On-water Delivery

- Instructor demonstration, with all students in the RIB
- Students try the activity two at a time, positioned either side of the RIB or in an area in front
- Students rotate in 10–15-minute cycles
- Avoid following students when foiling

The above is an ideal first-experience session. It allows the maximum number of students to take part on a minimum number of foils. It also takes into account the likely high fatigue of first-time foil students.

Safety Brief

Remember the number-one rule of foiling: KEEP HOLD OF THE BOOM!

If you look at most crashes where the student runs the risk of hitting the foil, keeping hold of the boom would have enabled them to remain clear of it.

If students try to dive away from their kit, they are more likely to cause impact and potential damage to themselves or the foil.

Teaching Points

Kit Setup Teaching Points:

- Foil anatomy, parts, and assembly
- Footstrap setup; tuning for different foils
- Mastfoot placement; mirrors lift of foil
- Boom height and line length; outhaul. Concentrate on its importance and also why it affects the rig
- Pre-flight checks

Launching Teaching Points:

- Carrying the board foil-first
- Safe depth for foils: chest deep. Think about the board volume and whether it will sink after launching
- Awareness of underwater obstacles
- Uphauling rather than beachstarting; having a continual awareness of where the foil is
- Reinforce rule number one: always keep hold of the boom. Hold the boom at all times to stay clear of the foil

Basic Takeoff:

1. Safety: keep hold of the boom, sheet out and move forward to avoid foiling and to stop. Uphaul where possible.
2. Wind/sailing angles: maintaining a sailing line, head off the wind and then head up to encourage a flat board. Sail just off the wind to build board speed.
3. Encouraging flight: front foot into the strap early, then put the back foot in the strap when possible. Weight the back foot to drive pressure through the foil, stay unhooked, pump the sail if required.
4. Sail position: unhooked to start. Keep the rig upright. Once in flight, keep the rig as still as possible.
5. Head position: look off the wind to help build speed, then look upwind to encourage flight.
6. Hands: keep the rig upright and away. Keep sliding the front hand forwards and backwards, which will help with the initial height control. Keep hold of the boom.
7. Hips: stay out of the harness, but with hips kinked outboard to keep upper body still and legs still able to trim. Move weight back to help induce lift.

8. Heels: lock the back heel down once in flight. Straighten legs, which will help keep a flat board.

9. Pumping: transition from rig pumping to board pumping, using the legs not the arms.

Landing or Stopping:

1. Techniques for controlling the landing; look upwind and sheet out a little on the landing.

2. Weight can then come forwards to reduce the chance of taking off again.

Landing on Shore:

1. Foil draft.

2. Carrying kit assembled; invert the board, using the mast as the contact point to carry.

3. Underwater obstacles.

4. Shallow-water approach; approach non-planing and non-foiling.

By the end of this course, the students will have an understanding of windfoiling, be able to set up, launch, and recover foiling equipment, and make their first short flights on the foil. They will have a basic understanding of the equipment available and opportunities for continuing, including the RYA Sustained Flights Course.

RYA Sustained Flights

Aim

This course aims to increase confidence and comfort surrounding the practical techniques and theory required to foil, steer, and maintain a course more effectively, as well as maintaining longer foiling glides.

Recommended course duration: Sixteen hours.

Students: Up to six.

Foils: Up to six.

Instructor: One.

Powerboat: One.

Session Considerations

The students have some control here, but your session should be set up in a way that tries to keep them from crossing paths. Stick to designated sides of the powerboat and away from other craft. More space is needed to windward as the students are likely to progress upwind.

Consider remaining anchored, with students returning to you for feedback. This means you avoid following students in a powerboat when foiling.

You don't need to have all students on kit. Conditions and ability may dictate how many sets of kit you have running throughout the session.

Teaching Points

Sustained Flight

1. Board trim: back heel locked down to maintain side-to-side trim.
2. Height control: front hand can move back and forward to help reduce or increase height. Weighting the front foot on the deck will help to bring the nose down and change the ride height.
3. Use of harness: hips set aggressively out with an upright body.
4. Kit setup: smaller straps may aid flight. Increase the boom height as this will bring the student more over the board.

Upwind and Downwind

1. Head: the head still controls the sailing line.
2. Hands: adjust the hand position to help change the height while on the foil.
3. Hips: shift the hips out to windward for upwind. Shift the hips back and forward to control the height downwind.
4. Feet: the back foot controls the trim; the front foot controls the direction.
5. Ride height: increase the height while going upwind but reduce the height for going downwind.
6. Wind/sailing angle: upwind, the sail will be sheeted over the centreline. Downwind, build speed before you bear away.

By the end of this course, students will be able to set up and tune their equipment to assist their foiling performance. They will be able to take off, sustain flight, and trim the board effectively, developing the ability to head on different points of sail.

Quick-look Fault Finding

Problem	Symptoms	Coaching/Solution	Kit Setup
Falling to leeward	Not maintaining a flat board when foiling, most likely because of legs bending in takeoff, or arms pulling on the boom while coming up	Focus on straighter legs and especially the back heel to control the tilt of the board. Lock arms or try underhand front hand	Footstraps too big. Board too narrow for wing or mast length
Spinning to windward	Too much lift through the back foot	Reduce lift by moving weight forwards or putting more pressure on the front foot	Front wing too big. Mastfoot too far back
Excessively weighted back foot	Lift is too far back	Encourage sheeting rig in more when getting lift	Either adjust foil angles, or move straps and possibly mastfoot back on board
Failing to foil	Not enough lift. Poor pumping technique	More weight needed on the back foot. Increase board speed	Tuning of rig may well be over outhauled. Wing and rig size may be an issue
Dropping out of harness lines	Hips and midline lifting	Encourage hips to push out and maintain a straight back	Shorten harness lines. Raise boom height
Can't maintain foil height	Not trimming for gusts. Legs bending in gusts	Begin by sliding front hand back and forwards to help pull nose down. Also focus on the fact that the front foot helps control height and the back foot controls tilt from side to side	Reduce size of footstraps for more control. Make sure rig isn't too flat
Catapulting on landing	Lift too far forwards	Make sure both feet are in straps when getting up	Move straps forwards as well as mastfoot

THE WING TEACHING SCHEME

Learn to Wingsurf

This is the first course in the RYA Wing Scheme, providing the basic introduction to wingsurfing. It sets the foundations that enable students to take the next steps of achieving first foiling takeoffs and glides.

There are no prerequisites. However, knowledge in wind-sports and/or foiling will accelerate the student's progression.

By the end of this course the student will have a good understanding of the equipment used and recommended, how to launch and land safely, and be able to perform a self-rescue. Initially, they will learn how to fly and control the wing on land, progressing to a board without a hydrofoil, before introducing a foil in the Wingfoiling First Flights course once ready.

This introductory course, Learn to Wingsurf, is split into two parts. Combined, they should last approximately four hours.

    a. Flying the Wing Ashore
    b. Wingsurfing Afloat

1. Learn to Wingsurf, Part a: Flying the Wing Ashore

Practical

Equipment and setup: Wing of 3m²–5.5m² depending on wind speed and student size. It is easier with a well-powered smaller wing.

Conditions: 8–25 knots.

Teaching ratio: 1:4 max.

Safety: This session should be done in an open area with space downwind and a consistent breeze. Use a small wing to ensure students do not get overpowered.

Aim: This session is to provide students with a basic understanding of how to fly the wing in a safe and controlled environment.

Introduction to Kit

Instructors may choose to split up the introduction to the wing and board and place them in at a relevant time to keep a logical flow to their sessions.

- How to pump up a wing, ensuring the wing is attached to either the pump or the person
- Parts of the wing
- Safe and secure leash attachment. Consideration of leashes should be discussed. If on flowing water, a waist leash should be used
- Introduction to the board (nose, tail, centreline, daggerboard etc.)
- How to carry kit
- Leaving the wing (once inflated) securely ashore

A front-hand and back-hand explanation needs to be included here, with reference to a board and its orientation.

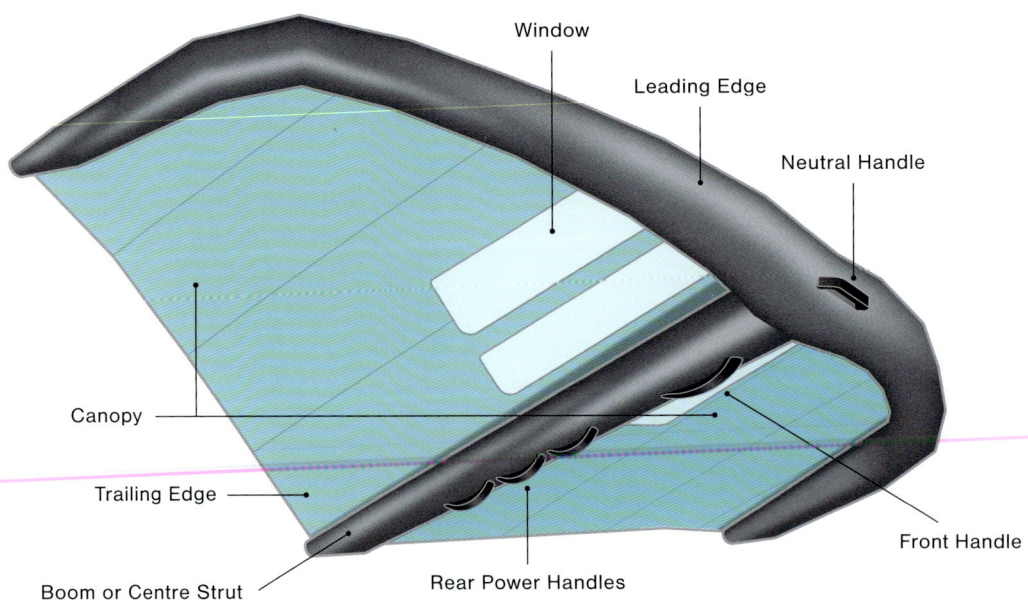

Session Considerations

This is to be taught on land, ideally in plenty of space with clean wind on a safe surface, giving the students time and space to practise, ideally with a consistent breeze. If required, use a smaller wing to ensure students do not get overpowered. When comfortable, students should be encouraged to do some 'wing walking' to allow them to build wind awareness and reinforce what they have learnt. The wing will behave and feel more natural when they are moving. Consider laying a course, as this will provide the students with points to aim for, as well as assisting group control.

The use of a beach board at certain points is also recommended to allow the students to orientate themselves with their front hand, back hand, and their ideal stance on a board.

Neutral Position

Aim: For students to understand how the wing flies and behaves in the **Neutral Position,** gain wind awareness, and reinforce the leading edge in relation to the wind.

1. With the leash firmly attached and feet shoulder-width apart, with your back to the wind, place your back hand (the hand furthest away from the direction of travel) on the neutral handle.
2. Lift the wing so it is flying freely. The higher the wing is lifted, the more easily it will fly.
3. The wing will fly with the leading edge into the wind, either upside down or the right way up.
4. When moving and carrying kit, the wing should remain in the **Neutral Position**.

Flipping the Wing

Aim: For students to be able to flip the wing without the wing tips touching the ground and understand the importance of front hand and back hand. Students should practise both ways.

1. Start from the **Neutral Position**, facing the wing, with the wind on your back and the back hand on the neutral handle, palm facing up.
2. Reach down the leading edge of the wing with your front hand.
3. Lift the wing high with the neutral handle and push the leading edge down and across your body with your front hand so your arms become crossed.
4. Allow the wing to flip over with the help of the wind. The higher the wing is lifted, the more easily the wing will flip.
5. Once the wing is flipped, remove the front hand from the leading edge and return to the **Neutral Position**.

Starting Position

Aim: To be comfortable transitioning from the **Neutral Position** to the **Starting Position** with correct and swift hand movements, understanding the importance of a goal point, knowing how to create power gently and how to release it. The use of a beach board is optional but recommended.

1. If using a beach-board simulator, keep your weight on the centreline, placing your back foot behind the daggerboard and your front foot pointing forward in front of the daggerboard. Turn your shoulders towards a goal point across the wind and drop your weight onto a flexed back leg while holding the wing in the **Neutral Position**.
2. Lifting the wing high above your head with an extended back arm, reach and place your front hand on the furthest forward power handle on the strut. If using a boom, place hand towards the leading edge.
3. Release the back hand from the neutral handle and place it swiftly onto a power handle towards the end of the strut or boom.
4. With the wing high and the leading edge pointing into the wind, this is the **Starting Position**.
5. To increase power and lift, pull down gently with the back hand. To release power, ease out with the back hand.
6. To return to the **Neutral Position**, keeping the wing high, release your back hand and place it onto the neutral handle.
7. Release your front hand and lower the wing into the **Neutral Position**.

Session Progression

While facing downwind and with the wing flying in the **Neutral Position**, gently shift the wing from left to right and see how it encourages rotation of the body in the opposing direction.

Powered Position

Aim: To manoeuvre the wing into a position that creates forward drive, and maintain a stable stance when power increases and decreases.

1. From the **Starting Position**, with your feet and body in the stable stance and your shoulders facing your goal point across the wind, pull down gently with the back hand.
2. At the same time, lower the front hand forwards in the direction of travel.
3. Keep your weight on a flexed back leg to maintain control. Continue to look at your goal point.
4. This is the **Powered Position**.
5. To stop, release your back hand and return to the **Neutral Position** via the **Starting Position**.

Session Progression

Wing-walking ideas (if space allows):

- Walk in a straight line in the powered position
- Copy the Instructor
- Mexican wave of wing flips
- Follow the leader

Leaving Equipment Securely Ashore

It is important that the student is shown how to carry the wing safely, both on its own and with the board, when it is introduced. The method of leaving the kit securely ashore should also be clearly demonstrated, weighting the wing down with the board.

Learn to Wingsurf, Part b: On Water

Students: Four.

Sets of kit: Up to Four.

Instructors: One.

Powerboat: Available and ready to go, as in the early stages beginners spend a lot of time drifting downwind.

Session Considerations

If not already done, the Instructor will need to introduce the board, its key parts, and how to carry and launch both board and wing together.

Wingsurfing is best taught in shallow water. If this is not possible, a powerboat will be needed. The smallest possible area should be used to enable feedback and instruction but also to help control the group.

Equipment:

- **Wing:** 4m²–5m², dependent on conditions and students. Smaller wings may be used if needed.
- **Board:** Use a stand-up paddleboard (SUP) with a daggerboard, or beginner windsurf board with centreboard (roughly 180L–240L), and a wing under 5m². It is easier with a well-powered smaller wing.
- **Leashes:** Suitable leash for the wing to be worn at all times unless instructed. Wing and board are not to be attached to the same place. Two coiled leashes are not to be used together.

Conditions: 8–25 knots.

Sea State: Flat. Maximum chop of 1ft.

Safety: Students must be in buoyancy aids.

Self-Rescue

The Instructor should give an explanation and demonstration of an effective self-rescue technique for the location and conditions.

Safety

- The quickest self-rescue method is to lie in a prone position on the board and paddle to safety, not worrying about the wing. This is only suitable for short distances.
- **To self-rescue further distances**, turn the wing upside down and manoeuvre it to the tail of the board, positioning one foot either side of the boom (or centre strut), hooking the ankles over the wing's leading edge.
- With feet pinched together, securing the wing, paddle to safety by lying in the prone position on the board.
- If using a short wing leash, attach it to an ankle for security during longer paddles.

A full deflation of the wing is also worth discussing, demonstrating how to deflate practically before resealing so the water does not get into the bladder.

Basic 180-degree Turn

Aim: To be able to turn the board through 180 degrees either towards or away from the wind.

To perform a basic turn:

1. From a **Neutral Position**, check the area you wish to turn in is clear of obstructions.
2. To initiate a turn, holding the neutral handle with the back hand, reach down and place the front hand on the leading edge of the wing.
3. Guide the wing towards the back of the board, keeping arms extended away from you.
4. As the board turns towards the wind, keep guiding the wing over the back of the board, at the same time rotating your body by either shuffling on your knees or taking small steps if standing, keeping your back to the wind and weight over the centreline.
5. Continue until the board has turned 180 degrees.
6. Ensure the board is back across the wind with the leading edge of the wing parallel to the board. Swap your new back hand onto the neutral handle.

Note: This demonstration can be altered and used to show a turn away from the wind if required, which some students may find easier at first. Remember to swap the hand on the neutral handle prior to the turn.

Session Progression

- For a tighter turn, shuffle weight towards the back of the board as the turn is initiated.
- To aid the balance and control of the wing, place the other hand on the leading edge.

Kneeling Across the Wind

Aim: To demonstrate the key winging positions to enable the students to wing towards their goal point across the wind, turn around, and come back. Instructors may choose to skip the kneeling section and go straight to standing if the wind is light or students are struggling with kneeling. As soon as the students are comfortable on the board, progress on to standing.

1. With the wind on your back, wing downwind of you, and the board between you and the wing, climb onto the board placing both hands on the centreline to help you do this. You can push down on the leading edge of the wing to help balance.
2. Position yourself over the daggerboard (if applicable), body weight over the centreline and knees 45 degrees to the front of the board.
3. Choose your goal point across the wind. From the **Neutral Position**, bring the wing to the **Starting Position**.
4. When comfortable, move into the **Powered Position**, pulling the power on gently with the back hand.
5. You are now winging across the wind.
6. To stop, ease out your back hand and return to the **Neutral Position**.

Coaching Point

If wing tips catch the water, focus on keeping the wing high and pushing down with the back hand.

Standing Up

Aim: To demonstrate key wing positions to allow students to stand up in control and wing towards a goal point across the wind, turn around, and come back. Basic 180-degree Turn if the group dynamic allows.

1. From your kneeling position, bring the wing to the **Starting Position**, pulling on some power with the back hand.
2. When ready to do so, keeping your weight over the centreline, place your front foot on the board in front of the daggerboard, facing forward, along the centreline.
3. Keeping power in the wing, weight your front foot and stand up with your back foot, placing it behind the daggerboard (if applicable) across the centreline.
4. Keep looking at your goal point and move the wing into your **Powered Position**, simultaneously dropping your weight onto a flexed back leg.
5. Adjust your body and feet to a comfortable position.
6. To stop, release your back hand and return to the **Neutral Position**.

Steering

Aim: To steer the board towards and away from the wind, making small adjustments to maintain a controlled course to avoid any potential obstruction in the water. The Instructor should provide background knowledge on the Centre of Effort and Centre of Lateral Resistance.

To turn towards the wind:

1. Pick a goal point slightly closer to the wind and shift weight slightly onto the back foot, slowly bringing the wing back with an extended back arm.
2. Once heading towards the new goal point, return the wing to the **Powered Position**, pulling in slightly with the back hand to maintain power in the wing.

To turn away from the wind:

1. Look back to your original goal point. Keeping body weight low and pulling in gently with the back hand, lean the wing forwards and towards the wind with an extended front arm.
2. Once heading towards your original goal point, return the wing to the **Powered Position** and ease out slightly with your back hand.

Progression Session

While winging across the wind, see how moving the body forwards and backwards along the centreline can affect the direction of the board.

Improve Your Wingsurfing

Students: Four.

Sets of kit: Up to four.

Instructors: One.

Session Considerations

Wingsurfing is best taught in shallow water or from a bank. If this is not possible, the use of a powerboat will be needed. Instructors may choose to teach from kit if students' abilities allow. A suitably sized area should be used to enable feedback and instruction but also to maintain group control.

Equipment:

- **Wing:** 4m²–5m², dependent on conditions and students. Smaller wings may be used if needed.
- **Board:** Large volume with a central fin or daggerboard.
- **Leashes:** Suitable leash for the wing to be worn at all times. Wing and board should not be attached to the same place. Using two coiled leashes should be avoided. If on flowing water, a waist leash should be used to avoid entanglement.

Conditions: 8–25 knots.

Sea State: Flat. Maximum chop of 1ft.

Tacking

Aim: To introduce the tack, creating a more dynamic and effective turn through the wind with the use of improved steering. A land drill is recommended for students to understand feet and hands.

1. From the **Powered Position**, choose a new goal point closer to the wind and steer towards it. Return to the **Powered Position**, remembering to pull in with the back hand.
2. Check for obstructions.
3. Gradually dropping your weight low by bending the front leg, pull the wing towards and past the centreline of the board over the tail.
4. Once the front of the board has passed through the wind, bring the wing high into the starting position.
5. At the same time, bring the back foot forwards to join your front hand, with the student standing tall and the wing high (Pencil pose).
6. Step back down the board into your new stable stance, moving your new back hand back.
7. Drop your body weight low on your back leg and steer the board back across the wind.
8. Return to the **Powered Position**, pick a new goal point, and wing away.

Coaching Points

Adjust your foot position on the board so you are not too far forwards or back. Ensure the front hand is placed in an overhand grip, palm facing down.

Progression Sessions

Once students have reached competency at the end of Learn to Wingsurf, they could progress by exploring the use of transferring weight to assist with steering as well as using steering to assist with the entry and exit of the 180-degree turn.

Upwind

Aim: Making progress upwind and how this can be achieved by combining winging closer to the wind with the tacks already learnt. The Instructor should give background theory on upwind sailing:

- No-go Zone
- Points of sail
- Maintaining sailing line to make progress

Session Considerations

- Instructor provides background theory to upwind sailing:
  - Students given a clear example of the concepts of wind awareness and the 'no-go zone' prior to upwind simulator or on-water demonstration
  - Our sailing line helps us to make progress upwind

1. From a **Powered Position** across the wind, pick a goal point closer to the wind and steer towards it.
2. Once heading to your new goal point, return to the **Powered Position** and hold this course.
3. You are now making progress upwind.
4. Once significant progress has been made upwind, check for obstructions and tack.
5. Repeat this process until your upwind goal is reached.

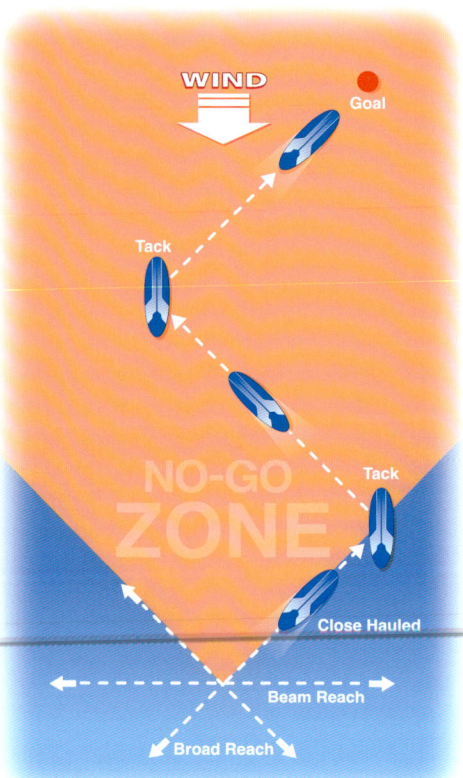

Switch Stance

Aim: To introduce the idea and movements of switch stance and how it can be incorporated into winging manoeuvres and general winging.

Going into switch:

1. From a **Powered Position** across the wind, steer yourself slightly away from the wind.
2. Lift the wing to the **Starting Position**, maintaining some power in the back hand.
3. Keeping feet on the centreline, bring the back foot forwards to replace your front foot. Step back with the old front foot.
4. Move the wing back into the **Powered Position** and keep weight low on your new flexed back leg.
5. To maintain your sailing line, keep your shoulders facing your goal point.
6. To switch back, repeat the process, ensuring the back foot comes forward first.

Progression Sessions

Experiment with the tack by entering or exiting into a tack in switch stance. How does it affect your balance?

Alternative Tack: From Switch Stance

On an upwind course, winging in a switch-stance powered position:

1. Turn the board into the wind by bringing the wing towards the back of the board.
2. As the board points towards the wind, bring the wing high and forwards into the **Starting Position**.
3. Release the back hand and swiftly swap hands (placing the back hand on the neutral handle).
4. The new back hand should now be placed on a power handle further back, keeping the wing forwards.
5. The wing is then slowly dropped down into the **Powered Position** on the new tack.

Gybing

Aim: To introduce the gybe and entry and exit variations.

Safety

- How to move the wing above the head to check downwind
- Basic Rules of the Road: windward/leeward, port/starboard

Gybing – Switch Entry

1. From a **Powered Position** across the wind, lift the wing to check for obstructions.
2. Ensure the front hand is in an underhand grip, palm facing up.
3. Keeping low, steer away from the wind.
4. Swap your feet into a switch stance.
5. Keep steering away from the wind, leaning the wing across the board.
6. Once on a run and as the board passes downwind, release the back hand and swap its position with the front hand.
7. Keep floating the wing to the new side, placing new back hand onto the power handle.
8. Continue to steer out of the turn by leaning the wing back.
9. Once back across the wind, bring your feet forward and return to the **Powered Position**.
10. Pick a new goal point and wing away.

Gybing – Exiting Switch Stance

1. From a **Powered Position** across the wind, lift the wing to check for obstructions.
2. Ensure the front hand is in an underhand grip, palm facing up.
3. Steer away from the wind.
4. Keep steering away from the wind, leaning the wing across the board.
5. Once on a run and as the board passes downwind, release the back hand and swap its position with the front hand.
6. Keep floating the wing to the new side, placing new back hand onto the power handle.
7. Continue to steer out of the turn by leaning the wing back.
8. You will now be in switch stance. When comfortable to do so, swap your feet.
9. Steer back across the wind and return the wing to the **Powered Position**.
10. Pick a new goal point across the wind and wing away.

Sailing Downwind

1. Lift the wing to check the area downwind is clear and free from obstructions.
2. Pick a downwind goal.
3. Steer downwind.
4. Return the wing to the **Powered Position** and ease out the back hand.
5. You are now heading downwind.
6. To turn, gybe.

Pumping

Aim: To introduce a basic pumping technique to help create power in the wing and increase forward motion.

A basic introduction to the technique for 'pumping' a wing, this will assist progression and effectiveness afloat, particularly during later courses when a foil is introduced. Depending on the student's ability and progress, it is a good idea to incorporate this power-generating method at an early stage. The Instructor should provide a demonstration on land and, if necessary, a demonstration afloat. Pump the wing by moving both hands in small circles: out, back, in sharply, then forward and repeat. Ensure the wing is kept high. The focus should be on a sharp inward movement. Throughout the movement, the wing should help create lift and therefore should still be slightly above the head, not down in front of you.

Success Measures

- The less noise the wing makes, the better
- Wings with a tighter canopy can handle a high rate of pumping
- Wings with a looser canopy require a lower rate of and pumping

The RYA Wing Scheme: Wingfoiling

The skills learnt for wingsurfing provide the platform for progressing on to wingfoiling and achieving your first 'foiling' flights.

Equipment and setup: A board with plenty of volume will initially provide increased stability for students. As a rough guide, it should be 40+ litres or more than their weight in kilograms. Please make students aware that this may not be the size of board they buy as their first board, but for maximising the chance of foiling and increasing control it is a good place to start. Footstraps are optional.

Wing size will vary depending on wind strength and student's size and weight, although a smaller wing will be lighter and easier to control.

The hydrofoil should be a low-aspect foil of 1,500cm² or larger on a mast between 75cm and 85cm.

Basic Foil Theory

Wingfoiling uses the same foil structure as windfoiling and prone/surf foiling. It has evolved to provide lift, balance, and control ride height through a single point of connection with the board. The 'T-foil' fits to the hull of a board in roughly the same location as a traditional fin, and is made up of:

- A mast
- Fuselage
- Front or 'main' wing
- Tail or 'stabiliser' wing

As the board gains speed and water flows over the foil's front wing it develops lift, causing it to rise towards the water's surface, elevating the board and thereby reducing drag.

The tail or 'stabiliser' wing helps balance the foil by stabilising the fuselage in the horizontal plane, much like an aft rudder.

The size and shape of a foil's front wing is carefully considered for winging. A larger wing will produce early lift at lower speed, enabling a wingfoiler to get going in lighter winds. The downside is that larger 'low-aspect' wings have a slower top speed. An advanced foiler may want to go faster, so may use a front wing with a smaller median/'high-aspect' surface area, at the expense of being able to get foiling earlier.

Mast: Produced in either carbon composite or aluminium, the length of the mast and cord varies.

- A shorter mast can be useful when learning to foil as it provides a lower riding position and gentler touch downs, but has reduced performance in rougher water
- A longer mast will allow for more space between the foil breaching and the board touching down, giving riders more chance to react to a change in height or wing power. On the downside, they may result in crashes from a greater height

Fuselage: The fuselage varies in length.

- A longer length increases ride stability but reduces manoeuvrability
- A shorter fuselage makes a foil more responsive, but less stable and more manoeuvrable

On most foils the fuselage can be disconnected from the mast for ease of transport and storage; however, some setups are one piece.

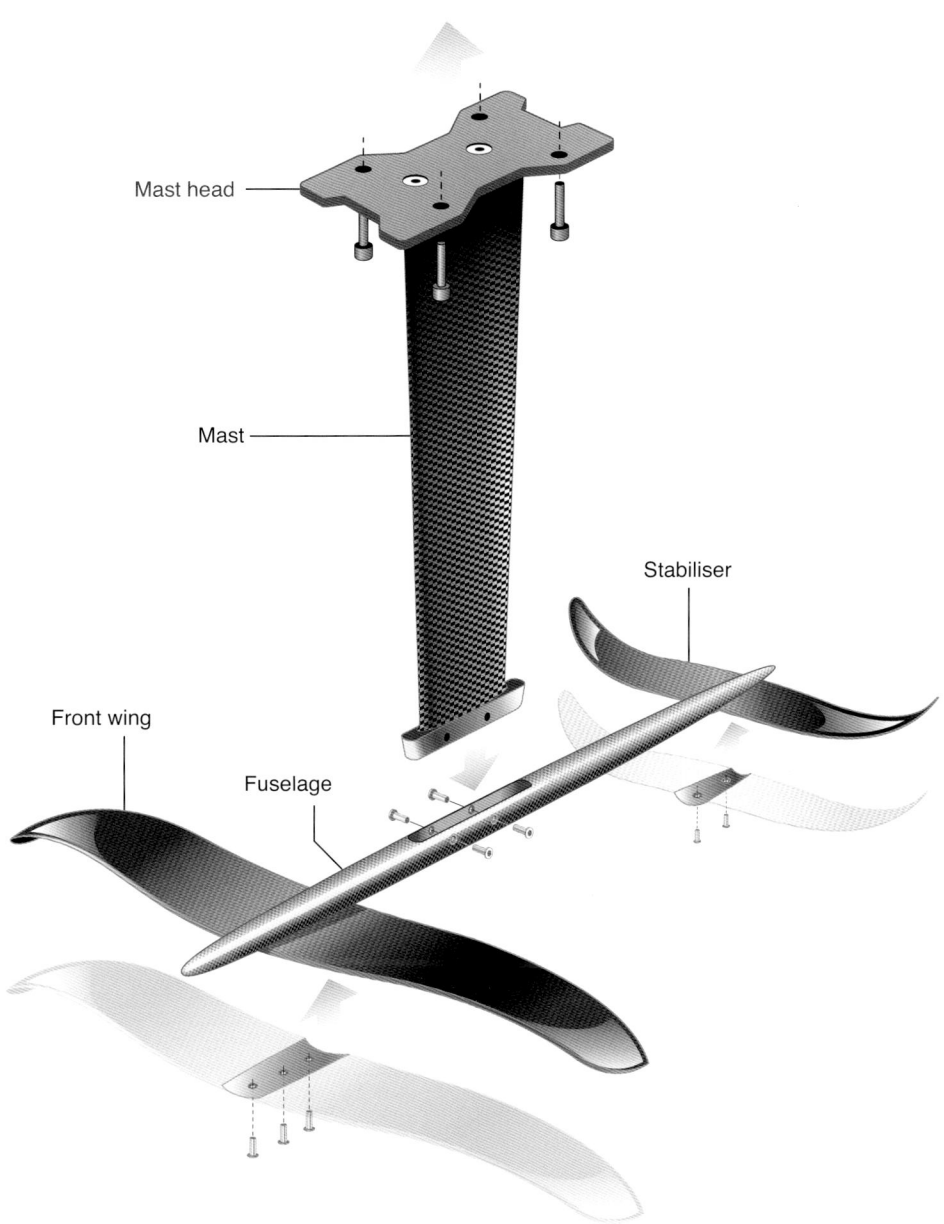

Mast head

Mast

Stabiliser

Front wing

Fuselage

Foil Wings

Front: The main provider of lift. There are two generic types:

- Low aspect: Often has the largest surface area, offering maximum lift at slower speeds
- High aspect: Work best at speed and offer improved high-end performance

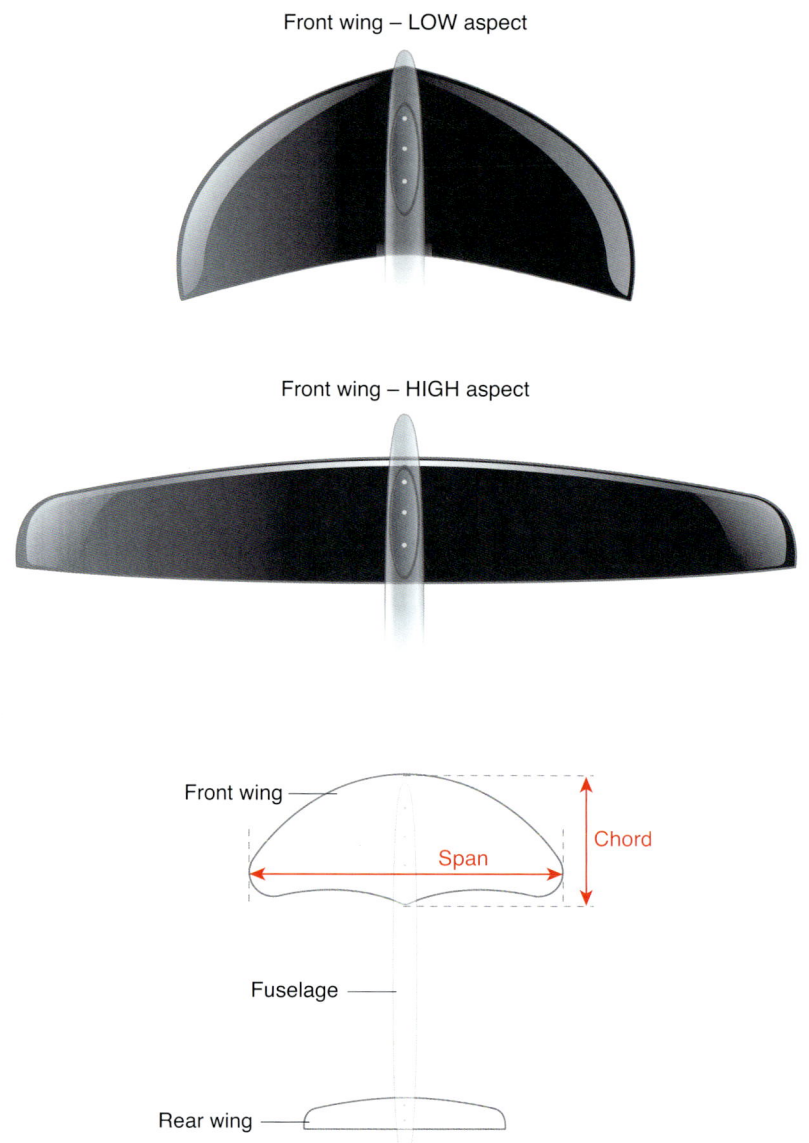

Front wing – LOW aspect

Front wing – HIGH aspect

Front wing

Chord

Span

Fuselage

Rear wing

Rear/stabiliser: Can be tuned for performance, depending on what the aim is.

- Large rear wings provide better stability and predictability
- Small rear wings enhance manoeuvrability and speed

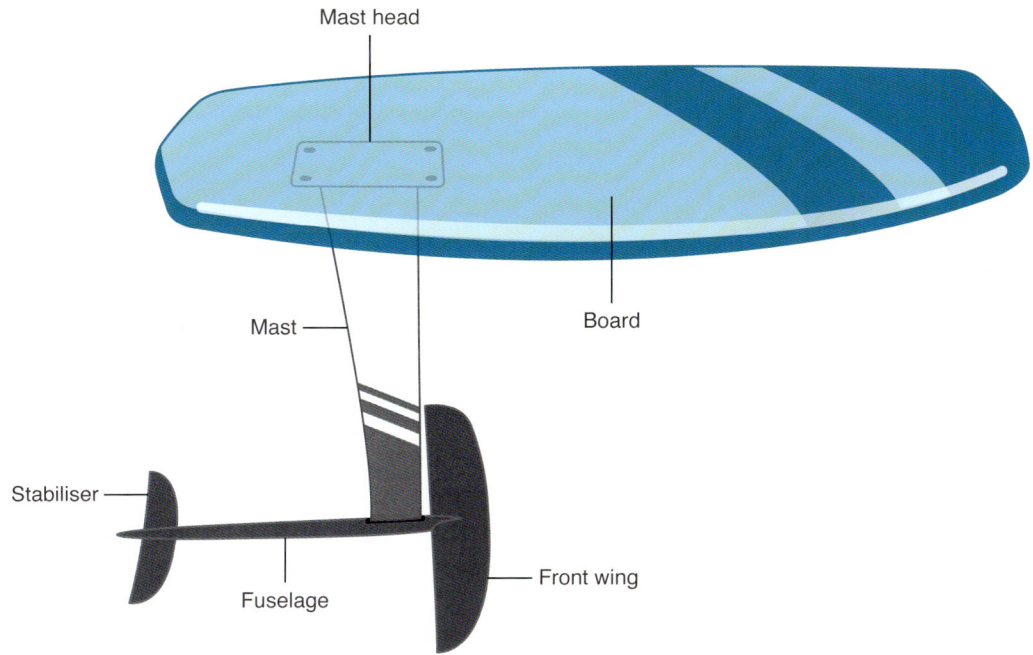

Mast head

Mast

Board

Stabiliser

Fuselage

Front wing

How the Foil Works

- As the front wing travels cleanly through the water it deflects water flow downwards, exerting an upward force on the foil
- This force creates higher pressure on the bottom of the front wing and a reduced pressure on the top
- This difference results in an upwards force, lifting the foil, and consequently the board it is connected to
- As the lifting force balances with the weight of the equipment and rider it will reach a point where the foil remains stable and the flight is sustainable with rider input
- The amount of lift produced by the foil can then be determined by altering the angle of attack of the foil via front and back-foot pressure

For further information see RYA Foiling (G110).

Wingfoiling

Session Considerations

The powerboat is to be used primarily as a coaching platform. Students should be of an ability where they don't require a huge amount of rescuing or towing back upwind. Lots of short sessions will allow students to rest, consolidate learning, and build up the skills and knowledge. A much-larger area and deep water are needed for these sessions as students will travel faster and a greater distance when up and foiling. For First Flights, reduce the amount of kit as students will get tired and it also allows them to watch and learn from their peers.

First Flights

Measures of Success

- Can ride the board off the foil
- Can get up on the foil and then come back down
- Can take off and land under control

Students: Four.

Sets of kit: Maximum of two.

Instructors: One.

Powerboat: One (you must teach from a powerboat).

Equipment:

- **Wing:** 4m^2–5m^2, dependent on conditions and students. Smaller wings may be used if needed
- **Board:** Suitably shaped wingfoiling board with a minimum 40-litre reserve volume
- **Leashes:** Suitable leash for the wing to be worn at all times unless instructed. Wing and board are not to be attached to the same place. Two coiled leashes are not to be used together
- **Foil:** 60–90cm mast (85cm is widely used) with a low-aspect front wing of between 1,600cm^2 and 2,400cm^2. Front-wing size will depend on conditions and rider

Conditions: 12–30 knots.

Sea State: Flat and deep. Maximum chop of 1ft.

Safety: Students must be in either buoyancy aids or impact vests rated 50N and helmets.

Launching

- Where possible carry kit individually to the water's edge, starting with the board, carrying it via the carrying handles while supporting the foil with the other hand. At the water's edge the board should be left upside down with the foil in the air and the nose of the board pointing into the wind
- The wing should always be carried by the neutral handle on the rider's downwind side

- Once at the water's edge the board should be closest to the wind and the wing downwind of the rider, who should be able to control both, positioning themselves in between the two
- Lift and slide the board gently into the water by lifting the foil from the fuselage, just in front of the mast
- Wade out into the water, with the board still upside down, until the water is beyond waist deep – deep enough for the whole foil not to touch the seabed while getting on the board. The wing can be released if necessary, maintaining connection through the leash, while walking the board out into deep-enough water

Returning to Shore

- When returning to shore, err on the side of caution and slow down early, climbing into the water to ensure there is enough depth for the foil
- Once a solid footing on the seabed is established, turn the board upside down and push the tail of the board towards the wind to ensure maximum distance between the foil and the wing
- Walk into waist-deep water before reeling in the wing and grabbing the neutral handle
- Pull the board close, lifting the tail out of the water by the fuselage
- If the board is secure in the water, carry the wing out of the water first, either securing it to a ground anchor or deflating it
- Return for the board and carry via the handles/foil

Safety

- Students tend to travel downwind quickly at this stage, as it is easier to generate speed off the wind
- The Instructor should have a safety boat ready at all times, setting strict sailing-area limits
- Falling positively during wipeouts creates extra distance between rider and foil
- Remind students that the wing can be let go as they fall
- Stress advantages of wearing a helmet and other personal protective kit
- Reinforce to students the silence of foiling around other water users

Aim

Generate small moments of flight. Bringing the board out and back down in control while gaining small moments of flight.

Key Coaching Points

- Head: Looking at a goal point across the wind or slightly downwind in more marginal conditions
- Hands: On the wing, maintaining constant power in the wing in the powered position
- Hips: Over and on top of the board to help maintain a balanced position, with even pressure over both feet
- Hooves: Even pressure across both feet. As soon as the board starts to rise, use slightly more front-foot pressure

If the students are struggling to take flight, the back foot could be weighted.

Progression Session

Once students are generating flight in control, progress to maintaining speed on touch down and then bring the board back up out of the water (bunny hopping across the water).

Sustained Flights

Measures of Success

- Can show a sustained 'run' across the wind with periods of controlled foiling
- A sustained flight looks like a well-trimmed board, coming back down smoothly off the foil rather than stalling or topping out

Students: Four.

Sets of kit: Up to four.

Instructors: One.

Powerboat: One (you must teach from a powerboat).

Equipment:

- **Wing:** 4m²–5m², dependent on conditions and students. Smaller wings may be used if needed
- **Board:** Suitably shaped wingfoiling board with a minimum 40-litre reserve volume
- **Leashes:** Suitable leash for the wing to be worn at all times unless instructed. Wing and board are not to be attached to the same place. Two coiled leashes are not to be used together
- **Foil:** 60–90cm mast (85cm is widely used) with a low-aspect front wing of between 1,600cm² and 2,400cm². Front-wing size will depend on conditions and rider

Conditions: 12–30 knots.

Sea State: Flat and deep. Maximum chop of 1ft.

Safety: Students must be in either buoyancy aids or impact vests rated 50N and helmets.

Aim

Maintain flight for a sustained period of time on all points of sailing, while controlling the ride height and remaining in control.

Key Coaching Points

While up and flying on the foil:

- Head: Looking slightly upwind
- Hands: Keeping the wing powered
- Hips: Use subtle hip movement to control the ride height. Legs should be flexed but not flexing
- Hooves: Planted with subtle pressure both front-to-back and heel and toe to maintain a flat board

Progression Session

'S' turns or very gentle flat-water carving, which will help encourage proactive steering.

Pumping the foil. While riding along maintaining flight and still powered with the wing, try pumping the foil with the legs. This will start to encourage the understanding of pumping the foil in more marginal conditions.

Improved Steering

With an effective stance and longer flights, the rider can start to concentrate on steering and making effective ground upwind and downwind.

A rider's vision initiates any change in direction and allows them to check that the area they are turning into is clear (by looking through the canopy window or bringing the wing above the head). It is then possible to foot-steer by applying pressure through the heel or toes of the back foot, and into the board and foil.

Bearing Away with Speed

Bearing away with speed is going to help gain confidence in going faster and give the rider the impetus required in the entry of the gybe, using their momentum rather than the power of the wing.

1. Look in the direction you wish to turn. As with any change in direction it is led with the eyes.
2. The rider should check the area they are turning into (through the wing window or raising the wing), as well as behind them for any other water users.
3. Confirming it is safe, they can initiate the turn by applying pressure to the leeward side of the board through their toes.
4. On larger boards a small half-foot-size step across to the leeward rail with the back foot will aid turning.
5. Pressure in the wing should be maintained by keeping the back hand pulled in.
6. As the board turns it will start to accelerate, at which point the rider may need to apply more pressure through the front foot to keep the board trimmed correctly.
7. To help maintain balance the rider can flex both knees and drop their hips a little lower.
8. As the board turns past a broad reach, the power in the wing will start to ease, signifying the direction of travel matches the wind's direction.
9. As such, the pressure through the toes can be reduced to slow the turn, aiming to go in the same direction as the wind-blown chop.
10. As the board starts to slow down, the wing will begin to power up again. Keeping their weight low, the rider can look to steer the board back across the wind, in the original direction of travel.

Learning outcomes are:

- Check downwind for clear space
- Bear away while keeping power in the wing
- Adjust weight to control the steering and trim of board
- Move hands to fly wing neutrally
- Either slow down and stop foiling or power the wing back up and head back across the wind

Changing Feet from Dominant to Switch Stance

In wingfoiling, the aim is to change feet and stance either before or after the gybe. Trying to do it mid-gybe will result in an untimely weight shift, which in turn will disturb the board's direction and make the gybe much harder. Initially, it is good to practise switching the stance across the wind while non-foiling in both directions. Starting from their dominant stance position, a rider must:

- Keep their eyes up, looking where they are going
- Consider briefly touching down, maintaining speed, skimming to assist the foot change
- Bring their back foot forwards, opening their hips to the direction of travel
- Move their front foot back, placing it across the board's centreline
- Ease the wing out with the back hand to reduce power

When moving the back foot forwards, it should land next to the front foot but slightly to leeward, meaning that when the front foot moves back onto the centreline there's a necessity to apply toe-pressure through both feet to help keep the board travelling in a straight line.

To return to the original stance, the above process is repeated in reverse. It is important to remember that the back foot always comes to join the front foot, not the other way around.

Controlling the Wing While Turning Downwind

Having practised bearing away with speed and turning back towards the wind, the next exercise is to turn downwind with speed, controlling the wing in a neutral position and using entry momentum to glide on the foil.

- Turn downwind in the same way as before
- This time, when the wing becomes light, it can be returned to the **Starting Position**, bringing it above the rider's head with their front hand, simultaneously easing out with their back hand
- At this stage the aim is to glide downwind with the front hand above the head and the back hand feathering the wing. Keeping the wing to the outside of the turn will help control
- As board speed is lost, the options are either to slow down until the foil loses lift, or to steer slowly back upwind, moving the wing down to leeward and gently bringing the power back on
- Once the rider is confident at flying downwind with a neutral wing, they can continue their turn and go past the run, being careful not to turn any further upwind than a broad reach on the new tack
- As they come past dead downwind, their back hand should release and come up the boom or centre strut to swap positions with their front hand
- The new front hand should stay high above the head, moving the wing towards the wind, establishing the **Starting Position** on the new tack. The back hand slides down to grab the power handle or boom
- Once the power is back on, the rider will be riding switch stance. They can now practise their switching-stance technique further by changing their stance from switch to regular while foiling

If the rider comes off the foil while gybing, they should continue to lean the wing to the outside of the turn to complete the gybe non-foiling before changing the feet once stable and comfortable.

Switch to 'Normal Riding Stance' Gybe

Having completed a gybe from a 'normal riding' body position to switch stance, the next gybe to try is from a switch stance back to a 'normal riding' stance.

The easiest way to set this gybe up is to gybe from a regular stance to switch, but not change feet positions before gybing back to the original direction.

Practising the same three points highlighted above (bearing away with speed, changing feet from dominant to switch stance, and controlling the wing while turning downwind), but starting from a switch-stance base will provide the necessary skill sets.

Other Gybes

While doing these two gybes will allow the rider to gybe in both directions and foil consistently, wingfoiling in a switch stance will limit performance. It is hard to power the wing up as effectively in a switch stance as when riding in a regular stance. It is also harder to point as close to the wind while riding in a switch stance. Learning to change stance from regular to switch and switch to regular on both sides should be practised. This will also help when it comes to learning the various foiling-tack variations.

Further Coaching Sessions

- Tuning kit for the conditions
- Catching chop and riding it downwind
- Foiling into tacks

BACKGROUND KNOWLEDGE & INFORMATION

RYA Organisation

RYA Training Centres

RYA Recognised Training Centres can issue RYA certificates in the disciplines for which have been approved. These centres fall into three main categories:

- Sailing centres open to the public
- Sailing clubs providing tuition for their members and prospective members
- Organisations such as local education authorities, Scouts, and HM Services, teaching their own groups or members

RYA Training Centre recognition is vested in the Principal. They are responsible for issuing RYA certificates and ensuring that the requirements of RYA recognition are maintained at all times.

Guidelines for the recognition of RYA Training Centres are available in a separate document from the RYA or from the website at www.rya.org.uk.

RYA Affiliated Clubs

Affiliated clubs have been at the very heart of the RYA since its foundation in 1875 and a large part of RYA work is still devoted to their promotion and protection. Any club with an RYA-specified boating interest may apply to the RYA for affiliation, namely:

- Windsurfing
- Dinghy sailing (cruising and racing)
- Yacht sailing (cruising and racing)
- Motor cruising
- Sportsboats and RIBs
- Personal watercraft
- Inland waterways

OnBoard

The RYA OnBoard initiative is aimed at children aged 8 to 18, making it super easy for them to get into sailing or windsurfing.

OnBoard is co-ordinated by the RYA and delivered all across the UK by RYA Recognised Training Centres.

Why? That's the easy part...

As we know, sailing and windsurfing are awesome fun, whether it's experiencing the mad buzz from going fast, getting competitive by learning to race, or just having a laugh hanging out on the water with friends.

OnBoard works alongside the RYA Youth Sailing and Windsurfing Schemes and has been making sailing and windsurfing safe and simple to get into for hundreds of thousands of kids all over the country since 2005. Whether near the sea, a river, lake, reservoir, or an estuary, there is an OnBoard club nearby.

The great thing about OnBoard is that kids don't need any equipment. All the kit to get started (boat, board, or personal kit) is provided by the centre. Children just need themselves; OnBoard does the rest!

Alongside teaching them sailing and windsurfing, OnBoard teaches them heaps of cool life skills too, focuses on developing creativity, confidence, teamwork, communication, determination, and independence.

The programme also complements the National Curriculum and supports a variety of valuable life skills that help to build confidence and shape personal development. Sailing and windsurfing can also spark a young person's creativity, improve their communication skills, and help them develop a growth mindset.

CREATIVITY

Creativity involves having good ideas, dealing with uncertainty, and being able to make links between apparently unconnected things. Creative people have made great discoveries through seeing connections where others have not.

CONFIDENCE

Being confident involves being a can-do person and being able to act independently. We gain more self-belief when we understand that making mistakes is normal, and know that the smart thing to do is to put in extra effort to work hard to improve.

TEAMWORK

Being a team player requires the ability to listen, show kindness to others, and give and receive feedback well. Giving helpful feedback is a difficult skill, but once learned it is very useful in many situations and an essential element of effective teamwork.

COMMUNICATION

Communicating well is very important. A lot of unhappiness comes from accidental misunderstandings or careless explanations. Communication involves learning how to offer opinions. It also includes how to match language to the audience or person receiving the communication.

DETERMINATION

Determination involves coping with difficulty. When we get stuck, we need to have strategies for getting unstuck! Sometimes we also need to know how to bounce back after setbacks, rather than giving up.

INDEPENDENCE

Independence is not just about learning to do things yourself. It's also about knowing how to get the best out of those around you. Becoming independent is a fundamental part of growing up, and includes making decisions and dealing with responsibility.

British Youth Sailing (BYS) Recognised Club

The BYS Recognised Club programme accredits and supports those clubs that have made a commitment to the development of junior training and racing-club activity.

They are safe and effective places to develop your skills and there will almost certainly be one in your area. Team15 clubs encompass the same values but focuses on windsurfing rather than dinghy sailing.

The process is run by RYA High Performance Managers. All details are listed on the RYA website. A BYS Recognised Club is required to:

- Provide a structured junior race training programme
- Guide their promising youngsters into the recognised youth classes following their period in a junior class
- Have sufficient numbers of a recognised junior class of boat or board (member or club owned), equipment, and qualified personnel to achieve the aims of partnership

The Duke of Edinburgh's Award

The RYA is recognised as a National Operating Authority for The Duke of Edinburgh's Award (DofE).

The DofE is a voluntary, non-competitive programme of activities for anyone aged 14–24, giving the opportunity to experience new activities or develop existing skills.

There are three progressive levels of programmes which, when successfully completed, lead to a Bronze, Silver, or Gold Award.

Doing Your DofE

Achieving a DofE Award can be made an adventure from beginning to end. Within an RYA Recognised Training Centre or club there are already many activities young people can take part in which can count towards their DofE. These could range from:

- **Volunteering:** Helping out at your local training centre, club, or Team15 night on a regular basis. This could be as an assistant, in the kitchen, or maybe even on the committee!
- **Physical:** Regularly taking part in sailing or windsurfing activity. Why not set yourself a goal to gain a certain certificate in the RYA National Sailing or Windsurfing Scheme, or maybe participate in regular club racing?
- **Skill:** All about developing your skills, whether practical, social, or personal. You may choose to sharpen up your powerboating, learn a new skill such as boat-repair work, become an Instructor, or perhaps increase your theory knowledge and learn all about meteorology!
- **Residential and Expedition:** You may never have been away from home before, let alone used your board or boat to go on an exciting adventure with friends, so now is the time!

Getting Involved as an Instructor, Coach, or Trainer

There is a considerable amount of interaction between the participants and the adults who are supporting them, with specific DofE roles such as Centre Co-ordinators, Leaders, Supervisors, and Assessors.

If you are interested in helping, further information on these roles or opportunities available can be found by visiting the RYA and DofE website.

- DofE website: www.dofe.org
- RYA website: www.rya.org.uk/go/dofe

Duke of Edinburgh Award Timescales

Bronze (14+ years)			
Volunteering	**Physical**	**Skills**	**Expedition**
Three months	Three months	Three months	Plan, train, and undertake a two-day, one-night expedition (At least six hours of planned activity each day)
All participants must undertake a further three months in the Volunteering, Physical, or Skills sections			

Silver (15+ years)			
Volunteering	**Physical**	**Skills**	**Expedition**
Six months	One section for six months and the other section for three months	One section for six months and the other section for three months	Plan, train, and undertake a three-day, two-night expedition (At least seven hours of planned activity each day)
Direct entrants must undertake a further six months in either the Volunteering or the longer of the Physical or Skills sections			

Gold (16+ years)				
Volunteering	**Physical**	**Skills**	**Expedition**	**Residential**
12 months	One section for 12 months and the other section for six months	One section for 12 months and the other section for six months	Plan, train, and undertake a four-day, three-night expedition (At least eight hours of planned activity each day)	Undertake a shared activity in a residential setting away from home for five days and four nights
If you didn't do Silver you must undertake a further six months in either the Volunteering or the longer of the Physical or Skills sections				

General Consideration: Advice and Guidance

Duty of Care

RYA Instructors and Trainers must always remember that they are usually teaching relatively inexperienced windsurfers who may not be able to make a sound assessment of the risks inherent in the sport. Instructors, and particularly Senior Instructors, should not hesitate to make prudent decisions in unfavourable conditions to ensure the safety of the students in their care.

Instructor Health Declaration

I understand that in my capacity as an Instructor I must be able to effectively deliver the relevant syllabus and look after the safety of my students.

Accordingly, I confirm that at all times I can:

1. Communicate effectively with students, other water users and the centre, and acknowledge that RYA Training is delivered in English other than at those centres specifically recognised to teach in Mandarin.
2. Recover other craft.
3. Recover a person from the water without assistance.
4. Keep an effective lookout by sight and sound and monitor the safety of vessels and crew within the session.
5. Operate a powerboat independently.

If for any reason, health or otherwise, I believe I may require support to fulfil the requirements above, I have provided further details below, which the RYA will use to consider what reasonable adjustments may be necessary to enable me to continue to instruct. I acknowledge that adjustments identified on the training course may be taken into account.

I undertake to:

a. inform the RYA if my situation in relation to the above requirements changes on a permanent or temporary basis.
b. submit a health questionnaire to be reviewed by the RYA doctor. In some circumstances a medical assessment may also be required.

Student Health Declaration

In order that they are informed as to any additional risk to students, RYA Recognised Training Centres are strongly advised to include a health declaration in their booking forms. The Principal/Chief Instructor must pass on such information to the individual Instructor responsible for the student.

The declaration should say that the student is, to the best of their knowledge, not suffering from epilepsy, disability, giddy spells, asthma, angina, or another heart condition and is fit to participate in the course. It should be signed and dated by the student and include details of any medical conditions or injuries and medication being taken. If there is doubt as to someone's fitness to take part then medical advice may be sought.

Swimmers

It is recommended that all those participating in the sport of windsurfing should be able to swim. No minimum level of swimming ability is stipulated, but students should be able to demonstrate water confidence.

It is essential that the Instructor in charge of a course knows if any course members are non-swimmers. Non-swimmers may be required to wear life jackets instead of buoyancy aids.

RYA Instructor Code of Conduct

The RYA values and respects the very talented people that make up our training network and views them as important ambassadors of the RYA's brand and values.

This document outlines the code of conduct to which all holders of RYA Instructor qualifications and RYA training appointments (hereafter referred to as Instructors) are required to comply.

The code of conduct is intended to make clear to all participants, Instructors, and RYA appointment holders, the high standards to which all are expected to conform.

Instructors must:

- Behave in a manner that is consistent with the values of the RYA, particularly with regards to equality, diversity, inclusivity, and sustainability
- Respect the rights, dignity, and worth of every person and treat everyone equally within the context of their boating activity
- Place the wellbeing and safety of the student above the development of performance or delivery of training
- Encourage and guide students to accept responsibility for their own behaviour and performance
- Only develop relationships with students that are appropriate and legal (especially those under 18), whether face to face or in a digital context. Relationships must be consensual, based on mutual trust and respect, and must not exert undue influence to obtain personal benefit or reward
- Ensure the activities they direct or advocate are student focused, and appropriate for the age, maturity, experience, and ability of the individual. Always clarify with students (and where appropriate their parents or carers) exactly what is expected of them and what they are entitled to expect
- Behave appropriately to ensure the safety of Instructors, students, and others under your direction
- Treat all RYA Instructors, appointment holders, staff, and other stakeholders with respect
- Act with integrity in all customer and business-to-business dealings pertaining to RYA training
- Read, understand, and comply with the Safeguarding Children and Safeguarding Adults policies and guidelines as detailed on the RYA website at rya.org.uk/safeguarding
- Comply with the laws and regulations of the jurisdiction in which they are operating
- Follow all RYA guidance and standards with regards to specific training or coaching programmes
- Not do or neglect to do anything which may bring the RYA into disrepute, including through the use of social media
- Hold relevant, up-to-date governing-body qualifications as approved by the RYA
- Only teach or provide RYA courses or RYA certification within the framework of an RYA Recognised Training Centre

- Notify the RYA immediately of any court-imposed sanction that precludes the Instructor from contact with specific user groups (for example children or adults at risk) and be aware that certain sanctions may result in the automatic withdrawal of your qualification
- Notify RYA Training in the event of any health issues that may affect their ability to carry out their responsibilities, including the use of medication which may impact their role
- Not carry out RYA training, examining or coaching activities while under the influence of alcohol or drugs

Failure to adhere to the RYA Instructor Code of Conduct may result in the suspension or withdrawal of RYA qualifications or appointments.

RYA Equality Policy

Policy Statement

The Royal Yachting Association is committed to equality of opportunity and aims to ensure that all present and potential participants, members, instructors, coaches, competitors, officials, volunteers, and employees are treated fairly and on an equal basis, irrespective of sex, age, disability, race, religion or belief, sexual orientation, pregnancy and maternity, marriage and civil partnership, gender reassignment, or social status.

Objectives

- To ensure boating is accessible and attractive to the widest audience
- To ensure that the RYA's services, including training schemes, are as accessible as possible, including to people with disabilities
- To increase the diversity of our Instructors, Coaches, and race officials
- To identify and promote more role models at all levels from under-represented groups, including women and girls, people with disabilities, people from BAME backgrounds, and LGBT+ people
- To attract new participants from under-represented groups through targeted initiatives
- To maintain the Advanced level of the Equality Standard for Sport

Implementation

- The RYA encourages its Affiliated clubs and organisations, Recognised Training Centres, and other stakeholders to adopt similar policies, so that they offer an experience to participants that is friendly, welcoming, and open to all
- Appointments to voluntary or paid positions with the RYA will be made on the basis of an individual's knowledge, skills, and experience and the competences required for the role
- The RYA will tailor requirements in relation to RYA training schemes which may inhibit the performance of candidates with special needs, provided that the standard, quality, and integrity of schemes and assessments are not compromised
- The RYA will develop further policies for specific subject areas where appropriate (e.g. instructing, race officials)
- The RYA reserves the right to discipline any of its members, qualification holders, appointees, volunteers, or employees who practise any form of discrimination in breach of this policy, in line with the relevant articles, rules, codes of conduct and disciplinary procedures
- The effectiveness of this policy will be monitored and evaluated on an ongoing basis by the RYA Safeguarding & Equality Manager reporting to the RYA Board and the Sports Council Equality Group

Avoiding Complaints

The best way to avoid complaints is to deliver training of the highest standard, covering the syllabus while offering excellent customer service.

Many complaints arise from a lack of communication.

After passing a course, students often wish to attend further modules. They usually haven't done any practice in between, so may not have the skills to pass. This should be recognised at the point of booking and appropriate alternatives offered. If not, the Instructor will need to do the adjusting and guiding. Fortunately, due to the scheme being modular, different skills, experience, and abilities can be catered for.

The purpose of the scheme remains to teach sailing and improve people's skills and techniques in a progressive manner. If the module is inappropriate the Instructor should discuss realistic aims and gain agreement using tact and diplomacy. Struggling students are often relieved by this process, with performance often improving once the stress has been removed.

- Ensure students are kept informed with regular debriefs
- Try to spot 'serial' complainers early
- Counter them by running the course 'by the book'
- Regularly ask them if they are satisfied, would like any further input, and seek agreement
- The Principal or Chief Instructor should also give opportunities for feedback as the course progresses

Helpful Advice

If a student is unhappy and this results in a complaint, any complaints received should be referred to the SI, Chief Instructor, or Principal (in that order).

Begin with *'Thank you for bringing this to our attention. How can we resolve it?'* Often more tuition is all that's required. It can save a lot of correspondence afterwards.

If you do not inform people of their progress you are more likely to receive a complaint along the lines of *'I didn't achieve the certificate because I wasn't taught well.'*

The Instructors who receive the fewest complaints are those who:

- Are competent
- Take an interest in their students
- Ensure that even the difficult or weak students feel they are an important part of the group

The instructional skills required are well beyond those of just sailing or even just teaching.

Manual Handling

Manual handling is any transporting or supporting of a load (including the lifting, putting down, pushing, pulling, carrying, or moving thereof) by hand or bodily force.

As an Instructor it is worth being aware that workplace injuries can affect your life and recreation as well as your work, particularly in later years. Injuries sustained while sailing can also affect your students.

This includes sudden injuries in the workplace as well as cumulative wear and tear commonly caused by poor positioning over a period of time. Common risks arise from:

- Excessive or awkward loads for one person
- Slippery or uneven surfaces
- Repetition or excessive duration of tasks
- Slipways, jetties, and dragging boats can all give rise to these circumstances

Studies show that the overwhelming proportion of accidents in the workplace are sprains or strains due to manual handling. Of these, back injuries are three times more common than any other injury.

The Manual Handling Operations Regulations 1992 contain guidance suggesting that manual handling should be included in risk assessments and that employers, employees, and volunteers should take sensible steps to minimise the risks.

Finally, when it comes to moving boats, ensure you have sufficient people to carry out the task safely, e.g. pulling a heavy dinghy up a steep slipway.

TOP TIP

Handling tips for Instructors:

- Widen the base of support while lifting/carrying
- Keep the load inside the base of support whenever possible
- Avoid asymmetry, e.g. carrying a heavy fuel can
- In general before lifting:
  ASSESS: task, load, environment, individual(s)
  PLAN: task, route
  PREPARE: load, self, area

Safeguarding and Welfare

Introduction

RYA Recognised Training Centres that teach children and young people aged under 18 are required to have a formal safeguarding and child protection policy which is checked as part of their annual inspection.

Your organisation is therefore strongly advised to take the following steps:

- Adopt a policy statement that defines the organisation's commitment to providing a safe environment for children
- Produce a simple code of practice and procedures governing how the organisation runs

The RYA publishes guidelines to help clubs, training centres, and Instructors to enable children and vulnerable adults to enjoy the sports of sailing, windsurfing, and powerboating in all their forms in a safe environment.

The policy, guidelines, and other best-practice guidance can be downloaded from the RYA's website (www.rya.org.uk/go/safeguarding) and adapted to meet the requirements of your organisation.

RYA Safeguarding Policy Statement

For England, Wales, and Northern Ireland this policy refers to anyone under the age of 18 as defined by the Children Act 1989 and The Children (Northern Ireland) Order 1995 and anyone aged 18 or over who is an 'Adult at Risk', who is in need of care or support, and who, because of those needs, is unable to always safeguard themselves as defined by the Care Act 2014. For Scotland, the act defines adults at risk as those aged 16 years and over who:

- are unable to safeguard their own wellbeing, property, rights or other interests
- and are at risk of harm
- and because they are affected by disability, mental disorder, illness or physical or mental infirmity, are more vulnerable to being harmed than adults who are not so affected

The RYA is committed to safeguarding all children, young people, and adults at risk taking part in its activities from abuse and harm and ensuring their wellbeing. The RYA recognises that the safety, welfare, and needs of children, young people, and adults at risk are paramount and that any person, irrespective of their age, disability, race, religion or belief, marital status, sex, gender identity, sexual orientation or social status, has a right to protection from discrimination and abuse.

The RYA takes all reasonable steps to ensure that, through safe recruitment, appropriate operating procedures, and training, it offers a safe and fun environment to children, young people, and adults at risk taking part in RYA events and activities. The RYA recognises that it has a legal responsibility to safeguard children, young people, and adults at risk, including due regard to the need to prevent people from being drawn into extremism and terrorism (the Prevent Duty).

The RYA is committed to minimising risk and supporting venues, programmes, events, and individuals to deliver a safe, positive, and fun boating experience for everyone by creating a welcoming environment, both on and off the water, where everyone can have fun and develop their skills and confidence. The RYA will treat everyone with respect, celebrate their achievements, listen to their views and experiences, and provide opportunities for all to fulfil their potential and be their authentic selves.

Through the RYA Training Scheme, the RYA is responsible for recognising Training Centres to deliver the RYA Training Scheme, and through its affiliation scheme, for providing advice and guidance for affiliated clubs and class associations. The RYA uses its position to require Recognised Training Centres to adopt and implement appropriate safeguarding policies and procedures and through its affiliation scheme encourages and supports affiliated organisations to do so by providing them with information, guidance, and support.

The RYA:

- Recognises that safeguarding of vulnerable groups is the responsibility of everyone, not just those working directly with them
- Carries out safe recruitment practices when recruiting all RYA employees, contractors, and volunteers in roles involving close contact with vulnerable groups
- Provides comprehensive training and personal-development opportunities for all staff and volunteers, irrespective of their position, to ensure that any concerns are reported in a timely manner and to the right person
- Responds swiftly and appropriately to all complaints and concerns both directly within and outside of the sport about poor practice or suspected abuse, referring to external agencies as necessary
- Provides signposting advice and guidance to anyone who needs it
- Offers basic safeguarding advice and guidance to anyone within the boating community irrespective of whether their club or centre is affiliated or recognised and gives full access to the safeguarding pages on the website to anyone wishing to access it
- Regularly reviews safeguarding procedures and practices in the light of experience or to take account of legislative, social, or technological changes
- Communicates changes and shares good practice with other NGBs, Recognised Training Centres, affiliates, and class associations.
- Encourages all RYA affiliates and class associations to adopt both a safeguarding children and young people policy and a safeguarding adults at risk policy.
- Ensures that all Recognised Training Centres have an in-date Safeguarding and Protecting Children and Young People policy which is in line with the RYA's
- Strives to achieve the highest level of safeguarding practices in line with the Child Protection in Sport Unit and Ann Craft Trust safeguarding standards and will undertake annual reviews of our policies and procedures to ensure full compliance with the standards
- Provides mental-health and wellbeing support to all staff through the colleagues' wellbeing programme
- Will co-operate where necessary with multi-agency investigations and inquiries relating to serious-case reviews involving children, young people, and adults at risk, if there is an association with the sport

This policy will be reviewed by the RYA Safeguarding Steering Group annually and by the RYA Board at least every three years, or sooner if there are relevant legislative changes.

RYA Recognised Training Centres are required to have a safeguarding policy that covers children and young people which is checked as part of their annual inspection. The RYA also recommends that RTCs should have a safeguarding policy and procedures that also covers adults.

Good Recruitment Practice

If a good recruitment policy is adopted, and safeguarding is covered in the organisation's risk assessment and operating procedures, the opportunity for an individual with poor intent towards children to gain access to the organisation or to abuse a position of trust should be minimised.

All applications, whether for paid or voluntary work, should be subject to an appropriate level of scrutiny. The level of checking you carry out should be proportionate to the role and the level of risk involved, and in line with relevant statutory requirements.

The risk is higher if the person will be in regular contact with the same child or children, in sole charge of children with no parents or other adults present, and/or in a role involving authority and trust, such as an Instructor or Coach.

The organisation should agree a clear policy and apply it fairly and consistently.

- **Who** to check:
    - Paid staff and/or volunteers (if they have the same level of responsibility and contact they should be treated in the same way whether they are paid or not)
    - New applicants only or existing volunteers/staff as well (if you are introducing checking for the first time you might want to start with new applicants and then check your existing volunteers or staff in priority order, depending on their role)
    - Those with specific responsibilities (e.g. Instructor, Principal, Child Protection/Welfare Officer, Coach, head of cadet section) or anyone who regularly helps with junior/youth activity
- The **level of check** to be conducted for each category:
    - References
    - Self-declaration (see RYA Guidelines)
    - Enhanced Criminal Records Disclosure (and Barred List check if appropriate) checks - The Disclosure and Barring Service for England and Wales, AccessNI for Northern Ireland and The Protection of Vulnerable Groups (PVG) Scheme for Scotland if the post is eligible

It is a criminal offence under the Safeguarding Vulnerable Groups Act 2006:

- For a Barred individual to work in Regulated Activity/Regulated Work
- For an organisation to knowingly allow someone who has been Barred to work in Regulated Activity/Regulated Work
- For an organisation to fail to make a referral to the Disclosure and Barring Service/Disclosure Scotland if they have dismissed someone from Regulated Activity/Regulated Work for harming a child or vulnerable adult, or placing them at risk of harm, or would have dismissed them if they had not resigned

Criminal Records Disclosure

Organisations affiliated to, or recognised by, the RYA can access the DBS (previously CRB), Access NI, or PVG processes through the RYA which is a registered Umbrella/Intermediary Body. The procedure varies according to the home country and legal jurisdiction in which your organisation is located. Full information is available from the RYA website (www.rya.org.uk/go/safeguarding) or by contacting the RYA Disclosures Team at disclosure@rya.org.uk.

Good Practice Guidelines

Culture

It is important to develop a culture within your organisation where everyone feels able to raise concerns, knowing that they will be taken seriously, treated confidentially, and will not make the situation worse for themselves or others.

Minimising Risk

Plan the work of the organisation and promote good practice to minimise situations where adults are working unsupervised or could take advantage of their position of trust. Good practice protects everyone – children, adults, volunteers, and staff.

These common sense guidelines should be available to everyone within your organisation:

- Avoid spending any significant time working with children in isolation
- Do not take children alone in a car, however short the journey
- Do not take children to your home as part of your organisation's activity
- Where any of these are unavoidable ensure that they only occur with the full knowledge and consent of someone in charge of the organisation or the child's parents
- Design training programmes that are within the ability of the individual child
- If a child is having difficulty with a wetsuit or buoyancy aid, ask them to ask a friend to help if at all possible
- If you do have to help a child, make sure you are in full view of others, preferably another adult
- Restrict communications with young people via mobile phone, e-mail, or social media to group communications about organisational matters. If it's essential to send an individual message, copy it to the child's parent or carer

You should:

- Never engage in rough, physical, or sexually provocative games
- Never allow or engage in inappropriate touching of any form
- Never allow children to use inappropriate language unchallenged, or use such language yourself when with children
- Never make sexually suggestive comments to a child, even in fun
- Never fail to respond to an allegation made by a child; always act
- Never do things of a personal nature that children can do for themselves

It may sometimes be necessary to do things of a personal nature for children, particularly if they are very young or disabled. These tasks should only be carried out with the full understanding and consent of both the child (where possible) and their parents/carers. In an emergency situation which requires this type of help, parents/carers should be informed as soon as possible. In such situations it is important to ensure that any adult present is sensitive to the child and undertakes personal-care tasks with the utmost discretion.

Responsibilities of Staff and Volunteers

Staff or volunteers should be given clear roles and responsibilities. They should be aware of your organisation's safeguarding policy and procedures and given guidance on:

- Following good practice
- Recognising signs of abuse
- Reporting any concerns to the appropriate person

Identifying Child Abuse

Abuse and neglect are forms of maltreatment of a child. Somebody may abuse or neglect a child by inflicting harm, or by failing to act to prevent harm. Children may be abused in a family or in an institutional or community setting by those known to them or, more rarely, by others (including via the internet). They may be abused by an adult or adults, or another child or children.

Physical abuse may involve adults or other children inflicting physical harm:

- By hitting, shaking, throwing, poisoning, burning of scalding, drowning, or suffocating
- Giving children alcohol or inappropriate drugs
- A parent or carer fabricating the symptoms of, or deliberately inducing, illness in a child
- In sport situations physical abuse might also occur when the nature and intensity of training exceeds the capacity of the child's immature and growing body

Emotional abuse is the persistent emotional maltreatment of a child such as to cause severe and persistent adverse effects on the child's emotional development. It may involve:

- Conveying to a child that they are worthless, unloved, or inadequate
- Not giving the child opportunities to express their views, deliberately silencing them, or 'making fun' of what they say, or how they communicate
- Imposing expectations which are beyond the child's age or developmental capability
- Overprotection and limitation of exploration and learning, or preventing the child from participating in normal social interaction
- Allowing a child to see or hear the ill-treatment of another person
- Serious bullying (including cyber bullying) causing children to frequently feel frightened or in danger
- The exploitation or corruption of children
- Emotional abuse in sport might also include situations where parents or Coaches subject children to constant criticism, bullying, or pressure to perform at a level that the child cannot realistically be expected to achieve

Some level of emotional abuse is involved in all types of maltreatment of a child.

Sexual abuse involves an individual (male or female, or another child) forcing or enticing a child or young person to take part in sexual activities, whether or not the child is aware of what is happening, to gratify their own sexual needs. The activities may involve:

- Physical contact (e.g. kissing, touching, masturbation, rape, or oral sex)
- Involving children in looking at, or in the production of, sexual images
- Encouraging children to behave in sexually inappropriate ways or watch sexual activities
- Grooming a child in preparation for abuse (including via the internet)
- Sport situations which involve physical contact (e.g. supporting or guiding children) could potentially create situations where sexual abuse may go unnoticed. Abusive situations may also occur if adults misuse their power and position of trust over young people

Neglect is the persistent failure to meet a child's basic physical and/or psychological needs, which is likely to result in the serious impairment of the child's health or development.

Neglect may involve a parent or carer failing to:

- Provide adequate food, clothing, and shelter
- Protect a child from physical and emotional harm or danger
- Ensure adequate supervision
- Ensure access to appropriate medical care or treatment
- Respond to a child's basic emotional needs

Neglect in a sport situation might occur if an Instructor or Coach fails to ensure that children are safe, or exposes them to undue cold or risk of injury.

Child sexual exploitation is a form of child sexual abuse. It occurs where an individual or group takes advantage of an imbalance of power to coerce, manipulate, or deceive a child or young person under the age of 18 into sexual activity in exchange for something the victim needs and wants (e.g. attention, money or material possessions, alcohol or drugs), and/or for the financial advantage or increased status of the perpetrator or facilitator.

The victim may have been exploited even if the sexual activity appears consensual. Child sexual exploitation can also occur online without involving physical contact.

Extremism includes people who target the vulnerable, including the young, by seeking to: sow division between communities on the basis of race, faith or denomination, justify discrimination (e.g. towards women and girls), persuade others that minorities are inferior, or argue against the primacy of democracy and the rule of law in our society.

Bullying (including online bullying, for example via text or social media) may be seen as deliberately hurtful behaviour, usually repeated or sustained over a period of time, where it is difficult for those being bullied to defend themselves. The bully is often another young person. Although anyone can be the target of bullying, victims are typically shy, sensitive, and perhaps anxious or insecure.

Sometimes they are singled out for physical reasons, such as being overweight or physically small, being gay or lesbian, having a disability, or belonging to a different race, faith, or culture.

Bullying can include:

- Physical pushing, kicking, hitting, pinching etc.
- Name calling, sarcasm, spreading rumours, persistent teasing and emotional torment through ridicule, humiliation, or the continual ignoring of individuals
- Posting of derogatory or abusive comments, videos, or images on social network sites
- Racial taunts, graffiti, gestures, or sectarianism
- Sexual comments, suggestions, or behaviour
- Unwanted physical contact

The acronym STOP – Several Times On Purpose – can help you to identify bullying behaviour.

Recognising Possible Abuse

It is not always easy, even for the most experienced carers, to spot when a child has been abused. However, some of the more typical symptoms which should trigger your suspicions would include:

- Unexplained or suspicious injuries such as bruising, cuts, or burns, particularly if situated on a part of the body not normally prone to such injuries
- Sexually explicit language or actions
- A sudden change in behaviour (e.g. becoming very quiet, withdrawn, or displaying sudden outbursts of temper)
- The child describes what appears to be an abusive act involving him/her
- A change observed over a long period of time (e.g. the child losing weight or becoming increasingly dirty or unkempt)
- A general distrust and avoidance of adults, especially of those with whom a close relationship would be expected
- An unexpected reaction to normal physical contact
- Difficulty in making friends or abnormal restrictions on socialising with others

It is important to note that a child could be displaying some or all of these signs, or behaving in a way which is worrying, without this necessarily meaning that the child is being abused.

Similarly there may not be any signs, but you may just feel that something is wrong.

If you have noticed a change in the child's behaviour first talk to the parents or carers. It may be that something has happened, such as bereavement, which has caused the child to be unhappy.

If there are concerns about sexual abuse or violence in the home, talking to the parents or carers might put the child at greater risk. If you cannot talk to the parents/carers, consult your organisation's designated Welfare/Safeguarding Officer or the person in charge. It is this person's responsibility to make the decision to contact Children's Social Care Services or the Police. It is NOT their responsibility to decide if abuse is taking place, BUT it is their responsibility to act on your concerns.

Handling an Allegation From a Child

Children may confide in adults they trust in a place where they feel at ease.

Always:

- Stay calm – ensure that the child is safe and feels safe
- Show and tell the child that you are taking what he/she says seriously
- Reassure the child and stress that he/she is not to blame
- Be careful about physical contact, as it may not be what the child wants
- Be honest and explain that you will have to tell someone else to help stop the alleged abuse
- Make a record of what the child has said as soon as possible after the event using the child's own words
- Contact the RYA Safeguarding Team
- **Follow your organisation's child protection procedures**

Never:

- Rush into actions that may be inappropriate
- Make promises you cannot keep (e.g. you won't tell anyone)
- Ask leading questions (ask 'how did you get that bruise?', **not** 'did X hit you?')
- Take sole responsibility. Consult someone else (ideally the Welfare Officer, the RYA Safeguarding Team, the person in charge, or someone you can trust) so that you can begin to protect the child and gain support for yourself

You may be upset about what the child has said or you may worry about the consequences of your actions. Sometimes people worry about children being removed from their families as a result of abuse, but in reality this rarely happens. However, one thing is certain – you cannot ignore it.

What to Do If You Are Concerned About a Child Or About the Behaviour of a Member of Staff

A complaint, concern, or allegation may come from a number of sources:

- The child
- Their parents
- Someone else within your organisation

It may involve the behaviour of a volunteer or employee, or something that has happened to the child outside the sport: perhaps at home or at school.

An allegation may range from mild verbal bullying to physical or sexual abuse. If you are concerned that a child may be being abused it is NOT your responsibility to investigate further, BUT it is your responsibility to act on your concerns and report them to the appropriate statutory authorities.

If you're not sure what to do and need advice, you can call the RYA Safeguarding Team on 02380 012796 Ext. 1 or the NSPCC's free 24-hour helpline: 0808 800 5000. Alternatively, you can visit the RYA's What to Do if You're Worried pages on the website (https://www.rya.org.uk/about-us/policies/safeguarding/what-to-do-if-you-are-worried).

INDEX

Note: page numbers in *italics* refer to illustrations.